SKILLS FOR
CARING

FAMILIES AND GROUPS

0443045283

ABOUT THE EDITORS

Susan Bird BA (Nurs) RGN CCNS CertEd (FE) FRSH

Susan Bird is a graduate nurse and depute head of department in James Watt College, Greenock. She was formerly Regional Coordinator for Open Learning, Strathclyde Regional Council and has taught in Further Education for several years. She is also a verifier in caring for SCOTVEC (Scottish Vocational Educational Council) and previously worked with SCOTVEC as National Development Officer for the Support Worker (Nursing) Programme and as a Project Officer for the National Health Service Training Authority (NHSTA) Health Care Support Worker Project and the Residential, Domiciliary and Day Care Project (RDDC).

David Rennie DYCS DSW CQSW

David Rennie is professionally qualified in social work and community work and has had extensive experience in social work as a practitioner, manager and trainer. He is a Mental Health Officer (Approved Social Worker) and helped design Strathclyde Regional Council's mental health training programme. He was seconded to the Care Sector Consortium to research and develop the new National Standards for social care workers and worked as a Development Officer with SCOTVEC. He is presently Inspector with the Inspection Unit of Strathclyde Regional Council Social Work Department which has responsibility for inspecting residential social work establishments across the statutory, voluntary and private sectors.

ABOUT THE AUTHOR

Robin Hall MA BD DipAppSocStuds

Robin Hall is Head of the Inspection Unit in Strathclyde Regional and is responsible for the inspection of all residential establishments in the region. He has extensive experience of institutional and residential life, having been an Assistant Governor in the Scottish Prison Service, Depute Head of an Approved School and Headmaster of a List 'D' School. His previous posts include Senior Lecturer in the Social Work Division of Jordanhill College of Education and Assistant Director of Social Work in Strathclyde Regional Council Social Work Department.

ABOUT THE OPEN LEARNING ADVISOR

Glennis Johnson BSc

Glennis Johnson is an educationalist with wide experience in Further Education and in the preparation and development of Open Learning materials. She was previously Programme Manager, then advisor and editor, to the Continuing Nurse Education Programme series of Open Learning Material produced by Barnet College.

ABOUT TERMINOLOGY

Throughout the text the recipients of all types of care are referred to as 'clients' and those involved in providing the care as 'care workers'. For simplicity, clients are always referred to as 'he' and care workers as 'she'.

SKILLS FOR
CARING

FAMILIES AND GROUPS

Robin Hall
MA BD DipAppSocStuds

Churchill Livingstone

EDINBURGH LONDON MADRID MELBOURNE NEW YORK AND TOKYO 1992

CHURCHILL LIVINGSTONE
Medical Division of Longman Group UK Limited

Distributed in the United States of America by Churchill
Livingstone Inc., 1560 Broadway, New York, NY 10036, and by
associated companies, branches and representatives
throughout the world.

First published 1992

ISBN 0-443-04528-3

British Library Cataloguing In Publication Data
A catalogue record for this book is available from the British
Library.

Library of Congress Cataloging in Publication Data
A catalog record for this book is available from the Library of
Congress.

For Churchill Livingstone

Publisher: Mary Law
Project Manager: Ellen Green
Editor: Valerie Bain
Production Controller: Nancy Henry
Design: Design Resources Unit
Sales Promotion Executive: Hilary Brown

Produced by Longman Singapore Publishers Pte Ltd
Printed in Singapore

The
publisher's
policy is to use
**paper manufactured
from sustainable forests**

Contents

© CHURCHILL LIVINGSTONE 1992 (COPYING BY PERMISSION ONLY)

To the reader

Here are some questions which may occur to you before you start to read this book

Who is this book for?
Anyone involved in caring. It has been designed with you – the reader – in mind. We've tried to make it look and feel friendly and attractive.

Do I need to enrol in a course to use this book?
*Certainly not, although you may find that it is used by many Caring courses. The books in the **Skills for Caring** series are for anyone involved in caring. You can use it on your own, at your workplace as part of an assessment programme if you're in employment, or as part of a more formal training programme at a college or other institution.*

Where can I read this book?
Anywhere you like. You can read it in 'snatches`, if this is more convenient for you, or you can interrupt your reading to do some of the exercises. It may help you to write on it, if it's your own copy. As you will see, the book has been designed to be used in a very flexible way.

Are there any special features that I should be aware of before starting to read this book?
You'll find it a great help to know the following:

Definitions:
*Sometimes a key word might be unfamiliar to some readers, or we might want to be sure that the **precise** meaning is clear. We've tried to pick out such words and give their meaning at the place where the word is first mentioned. The word and its definition have been set off in a box.*

Examples:
There's no substitute for a good example to make a point or convey a message. We've included as many examples as possible and have set these off from the main text with boxes, so that you can skip them if you like, or locate them again if you found them particularly helpful.

Exercises:
*These have been set off from the text in a different colour. The exercises can extend your knowledge considerably and reinforce what you've read in the main text. You can do the exercises on your own, with a group, or under the direction of a tutor. Or you can choose **not** to do them at all, or to do them later, after you've read and absorbed the text. The choice is yours. Remember: This is **your** book – enjoy it!*

Introduction

■ *This book is for people who will come into contact with families and groups in the course of their work or studies. It is not a book for specialists but is for anyone interested in understanding more about what goes on between individuals when they form a group.*

Throughout the book you are asked to draw upon your own ideas and experiences, consider a variety of situations and arrive at your own conclusions. You will find that there are no easy answers, only different ways of approaching certain circumstances.

Some of the ideas in the book may be quite new to you. You will have to think carefully before you can use these ideas effectively. Perhaps you will need the help and support of others – friends, tutors, fellow students or colleagues at work.

There are many theories about families and groups and about the best way to work with them. However, instead of commenting on these theories, this book concentrates on offering practical help. Through examples and exercises, it aims to increase your understanding of the ways in which the members of families and groups relate with one another and with their care worker. As the book challenges you to think about your own family and life experiences, you may find that some of the exercises explore questions which touch on sensitive areas.

The main aims of this book are:

- **to describe what underlies relationships between people, particulary in connection with their needs**
- **to develop an understanding of what happens in families and groups**
- **to suggest ways in which care workers can put this understanding to good use as they develop expertise in their line of work, study or interest.**

NOTES

NOTES

1

Working with people

'I like working with people.'

People often say that they choose to work in the field of health or social care because they like working with people. However, there are different *ways* of working with people. Someone applying for a job in a supermarket could also say that it is important for him to like working with people.

Both care workers and workers in a supermarket require patience, tolerance, sensitivity and the ability to see the other person's point of view. However, people do not expect someone who is a care worker in a children's home to approach her job in the same way as someone who works in a supermarket. A supermarket worker has to meet the needs of customers, but a care worker has to meet the personal needs of a client. Care workers soon find that being so intimately involved with another person's life is demanding and can be distressing.

So what are the *specific* differences between working with people in general and working with people in a more specialised setting, such as a children's home, hospital or training centre?

LIVING AND WORKING IN GROUPS

Clients do not live in isolation; they live in relation to other people. Clients also live in relation to the care worker. The care worker may feel very close to the group, but she must always remember that she is *not* a fellow member of the clients' group. Similarly, in a hospital, day centre or residential home, the care worker is a member of the centre but not part of the client group in the centre.

It is important to learn about, and understand, your client in the context of his own environment. As a care worker you cannot ignore the client's life experience and his surroundings, but you must remember that you are not part of the client's basic experience or lifestyle.

However, although you are not part of the basic environment of your clients, as you work with them you do affect their environment. For example, a care worker may help to put an elderly person or child in touch with his family again. This is not only because the worker has a genuine regard for the people involved, and can understand their differing points of view, but also because she is sufficiently separate from their problems to see things from a new point of view. If the care worker becomes 'part of the family' she could become so entangled with the family's affairs that she would not be of very much use to them. The family might even think that she was interfering.

You can think about this further by trying Exercise 1.

● ●

EXERCISE 1

Think of a client (or similar person) you have become very close to:
● **Do you like him? Why?**
● **Does he like you? Why?**
● **Do his relatives like you? Why?**
● **Do his relatives sometimes expect too much of you because they see that you and the client like each other?**
● **Do his relatives sometimes seem resentful because you are getting more attention than they think you should?**
● **Do you ever get the impression that his relatives think you are interfering?**

● ●

As care workers we must remember a few basic rules:

- **We are not a member of the client's group, history or experience of life.**
- **We must work within the client's own experience of life.**
- **We should be aware of the ways in which we influence our client's life.**

To keep these rules we need to understand:

- **What happens in people's lives as they go about their business with others and**
- **What happens when clients and care workers get together, whatever the setting.**

AUTHORITY AND LEADERSHIP

As a care worker you will encounter many different relationships between people and be involved in relationships with them yourself. All these relationships will involve the use of authority. 'Authority' describes the activity whereby people who are working together exercise their influence on one another. As care workers we have to decide *how* we exercise our authority – will we be **authoritarian** or **authoritative?**

AUTHORITARIAN

Most of us have experience of working under authoritarian leaders. These are people who are so unsure of their own personal and professional authority for doing the job that they make themselves feel more important by putting others 'in their place.' They want to remind people of their senior position because they are frightened of the possibility that other people might also have the authority to do their own jobs. Perhaps this also makes them feel threatened. Sometimes, this is called 'cap badge authority' and people react to it by saying 'All right, I'll respect the rank but don't expect me to respect the person!'

Now try Exercise 2.

EXERCISE 2

Think about a time when you were subject to an authoritarian leader or parent. How did it affect you? How did you respond? Did you:

- curl up in a corner
- 'lash out' in some way and get 'hammered down' again
- keep quiet and store up your anger and frustration inside
- decide to flatter the person in order to keep the peace
- show any other reaction?

The answers you give to Exercise 2 will be affected by many things, including your previous experience, your personality, and your surroundings and mood on a particular occasion. None of the responses is better than any of the others.

An example of authoritarianism is the way some adults behave towards children. This attitude is that children have no authority *because* they are children. If an adult believes he has all the authority how can a child exercise his own authority? Either he doesn't, and becomes compliant and withdrawn, or he 'kicks back'. There is no acceptable way for a child to 'kick back' so he has to choose other means and is soon labelled 'anti-authoritarian' (although you probably know children who have a grudge against authority however sensitively it is exercised!)

An authoritarian style seldom produces constructive responses from which real progress can be made in a relationship. Instead, the person who is being humiliated either gives a weak-willed response or secretly feels pleased, because he is responding in an anti-authoritarian way towards someone who is trying to belittle him.

AUTHORITATIVE

Authoritative leaders are confident of their personal and professional authority, as it relates to their job. They can, therefore, allow you to exercise *your* authority in relation to *your* job. They not only give you your rightful place, they *insist* that you have it. In other words, their attitude to you is 'If we are to accomplish the task we have to do it together, it is essential that we *both* exercise our authority. The task requires our differing knowledge and skills

to be used to the full, which is why I have asked you to be involved.'
See Exercise 3.

● ●

EXERCISE 3

Think about what it is like to work with an authoritative leader:
- Does she give you your place?
- What effect does that have on you? Does it give you more responsibility than you have when working with another type of leader?
- Are you pleased with more responsibility or are you sometimes frightened by it?
- Do you ever wish that your leader would be more authoritarian and tell you what to do?

● ●

The characteristics shown in the box contrast the two leadership styles.
Use the information in the box for Exercise 4.

● ●

EXERCISE 4

After reading the information given in the box, add further examples from your own experience of the characteristics displayed by authoritarian and authoritative people.

● ●

You may feel quite comfortable with your own authority at work, but if it is challenged (legitimately or not!) you may still find yourself retreating into an authoritarian role. You may pride yourself in always giving other people, juniors or seniors, their rightful place, but when challenged you retaliate with the words 'Who do you think you are talking to?' Exercising authoritative leadership is difficult and something you have to work at continually.

AUTHORITY AND 'FOLLOWERSHIP'

The idea of 'followership' is an important one because, however they get their authority, leaders don't get very far unless they have followers who are prepared to follow!

Every day we are surrounded by leaders of different kinds whom we warm to, resent or dismiss. *How* people follow a leader affects the way in which they achieve their tasks. For example, they may be meek and unquestioning followers, leaving behind their own authority. Or they may bring their own authority with them as they follow others. Yet just because we are followers does not mean that we abandon our own freedom to think for ourselves and make our own judgements.

We are still entitled to give expression to our own authority even in the position of followership – this is authoritative followership.

It is very difficult to put 'authoritative followership' into practice. Many followers give up their responsibility by saying something like 'Don't ask me, I only work here!' Also, it is extremely difficult to be an authoritative follower if your boss is an authoritarian leader who is intent on denying your own authority in order to assert hers.

If we are to have an open and honest working relationship with clients and colleagues then we must face the challenges of authoritative leadership and followership. These challenges are basic to the growth of the individual in personal, work or community life. In other words, taking authority

THE AUTHORITARIAN PERSON	THE AUTHORITATIVE PERSON
• Can only remain confident herself by making others feel less confident. • Relies a lot on her rank and position. • Treats juniors as if they have no authority of their own. • Reacts angrily, or is offended, when those junior to her assert themselves. Cannot handle constructive criticism. • Keeps people in their place by patronising those who are subservient to her.	• Is comfortable with her job and the authority which goes with it. • Does not have to humiliate others to express her own authority. • Welcomes and uses the authority expressed by juniors and other colleagues. • Is able to listen to, and act on, constructive criticism. • Is able to listen to, and act on, comments about the way she does her job.

for oneself, whether in leadership or followership, is a responsibility as well as a freedom.

Think about this further in Exercise 5.

• •

EXERCISE 5

The term 'authoritative followership' may sound odd to you.
• Write down what you think it means.
• Describe an occasion when you did a job really well because you were given your place and your leader made it plain what she expected from you.

• •

BENEATH THE SURFACE

In daily life things go on between people which don't appear to make sense. This is because of other things people won't admit to, or to which they are oblivious, such as projection and transference.

PROJECTION

Have you ever felt that you were being criticised for something about yourself which wasn't really part of you at all and that what you were being blamed for belonged more to the person who was attacking you than to you yourself? This is called **projection.**

Projection occurs when a person puts on to somebody else a characteristic – usually negative – which actually belongs to the person himself. The person then proceeds to attack the other for having that characteristic. It is as if we have such difficulty recognising the disagreeable bits of ourselves that we shift them on to others and then attack them for having the very characteristic which belongs to us.

Projection can occur in the relationship between client and care worker. If you have worked in residential care you may have experienced projection from the parents or families of your residents. For example, a family may feel guilty about arranging for their elderly relative to be admitted to a home for elderly people, rather than continuing to look after him in the family home. They might express this guilt by attacking the staff in the home for not looking after their relative properly when it is obvious that he is being looked after very well. Similarly, one or both parents of a

EXAMPLE

A nurse working in a geriatric ward became very fond of one of the male patients, but instead of welcoming a chat with members of his family when they came to visit she was quite abrupt with them. Her attitude upset the family because the old man told them how kind the nurse had been to him. The old man was upset too, because he liked the nurse and wanted his family to approve of her. As a result, both the old man and the nurse were confused because their straightforward, genuine fondness for each other had been damaged.

What the people involved in this situation didn't realise was that the nurse's parents had sent her grandfather to a residential home long before it was necessary. She had always resented her parents for doing this and was projecting her anger against them onto the old man's family.

child in a children's home may accuse the staff of negligence, but, what they are really referring to is their *own* negligence.

It is not only clients who project on to care workers – care workers may project on to clients. A care worker has to make sense of what the client may be putting on to her *and* be aware of any prejudices she may be putting on to the client. If she is not alert to this two-way process the working relationship with her client could go badly wrong, as the example above shows.

When you have read this example try Exercise 6.

• •

EXERCISE 6

• Can you think of occasions when a person has accused you of faults which you know belong to him or her rather than you?
• Have you ever found yourself criticising people for behaviour which you know is more like yours than theirs?
If you are able to think of examples to answer both questions then you are getting to grips with this strange but common aspect of people's underlying behaviour.

• •

TRANSFERENCE

If client and care worker have a close working relationship, the client may invest a range of very powerful feelings in the care worker. If they also spend a lot of time together these powerful feelings may affect the way the client behaves towards the care worker. The client is rediscovering feelings that he had for people – like his mother or father – who were very important to him in his early life. These feelings may become so powerful that he begins to behave towards his care worker as if *she* were that significant person. This is called **transference.**

This may sound far-fetched, but we can hear examples of transference in everyday phrases like 'He is the son I never had', 'She's been just like a mother to me' or 'He's my father figure'. The example on the right describes a situation where transference caused problems in a working relationship.

Now try Exercise 7.

● ●

EXERCISE 7

Make a short list of people who were important to you during your childhood. Include anyone who had a strong influence on your life, for good or bad reasons. Then make a similar list of people who are important to you now – family, friends, bosses you have worked for.

- Do you see any links between the two lists?
- Have you found yourself relating to someone in both lists in the same way?
- Is your behaviour towards someone in the second list affected by your experience of someone in the first list?

If your answer to any of these questions is 'Yes' then take some time to work out how your behaviour is affected.

● ●

It is important that you are aware of the influences underlying human behaviour. Without this knowledge you can become confused about what is actually happening between yourself and your client, especially if a relationship which started well begins to go wrong.

THEMES

'**Theme**' is a technical word used to describe certain aspects of a person's picture of himself,

---

EXAMPLE

A new psychologist started visiting a residential school every week. She and the headmaster immediately ran into difficulties. It was soon clear that they found it impossible to work together, but no one could work out why. In fact, the problem was that the headmaster reminded the psychologist so much of her own father, whom she hated, that she could not stand being near him. Eventually, she had to leave the unit because the connection between the headmaster and her father was too strong for her to overcome.

---

that is, part of his self-image. Themes refer to a person's attitudes to his own and other people's lives, his views about human relationships, and his ways of behaving toward other people (including whether or not he warms to them or draws away from them). It includes his assumptions about childhood, adolescence, sex, parenthood and growing old.

We all have our own themes – our preferences, prejudices and blind spots. As care workers, how is our work with other people's themes affected by our own?

A care worker uses her own life experience, and knowledge of human relations, to help understand what is happening to the client. If she did not bring her personal life experience to the relationship she would be denying her client any sense of her being a 'real' person – she would simply be carrying out the 'mechanical' parts of the job.

A client's concerns will have a profound effect on you and you must know how to manage your feelings.

INTERACTION: HAVING AN EFFECT UPON EACH OTHER.

The interaction of themes is part of the everyday relations between people, but it has to be carefully monitored in the more formal relationship of client and care worker. A care worker must not let her theme interfere with the help she is giving the client to explore his theme. She has to be a 'real' person to her client by acknowledging her own feelings. But she must not allow her personal view

© CHURCHILL LIVINGSTONE 1992 (COPYING BY PERMISSION ONLY)

of things to get in the way of listening to the feelings and views of her client.

In the example below the imaginary conversation between two mothers shows 'theme interference' at work.

Senga and Betty are listening to one another, but what each says sparks off something in the other's theme or preoccupation. Instead of dealing with the issues one at a time they are caught up in their own themes – so neither of them gets anywhere!

Try Exercise 8.

- -

EXERCISE 8

Think of some occasions when you've wanted to say something important. You have taken your courage in both hands and started when someone interrupts, saying things like:

- **'I know what you mean. I've got the answer for you. This is what you should do...'**
- **'You think you've got problems? That's nothing! Wait till you hear what I've got to tell you...'**
- **'Stop. I don't think we should be talking about such things because it is very upsetting. Let's talk about something else.'**

You have been left 'up in the air'; your theme has been interfered with, or stopped. How did you feel about this?

Now try to think of times when someone started to speak about something he really wanted to talk about and *you* jumped in too fast with your own ideas.

- -

EXAMPLE

Senga: 'I really don't know what to do, Betty. I'm going round the twist with worry about our Angie. She's only 16 and she's out every night till goodness knows when. I've no idea where she goes and who she's with. She never tells me anything. I'm terrified she's in with the wrong kind of friends and will get into real trouble...'

Betty: 'That's terrible, Senga, but you should hear about my husband. He's a layabout. He stays in bed all day and goes out drinking all night. Last night he came back with a terrible gash on his face and then the police banged on the door at 3 in the morning. You think you've got problems!'

Senga: That's awful, right enough. But what will I do with our Angie?'

Betty: See that John. If he goes on like this I'll kill him.'

You will realise from Exercise 8 that 'theme interference' is something we all do as part of daily life, but in our work we need to be more careful about not doing it to clients.

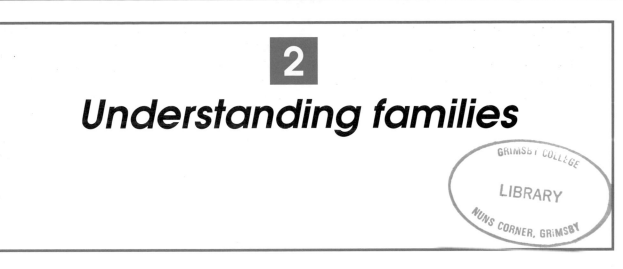

2

Understanding families

■ Although people's experience of living in families varies enormously – some people may not experience any family life at all – most will have an idea of what family life could, or should, be.

When we think about what happens in families we are influenced by what happened in our own families. It is important to use these ideas about family life in our learning, but we must not let our personal experiences (or 'themes') prevent us from expanding our knowledge about other people's families. As a care worker, you will find differences as well as similarities between your experience of families and the experience of the families you work with. Remember, each family is unique and that uniqueness needs to be respected.

Living in family groups has always been considered one of the best ways of meeting people's basic personal needs. Everyone has needs which continue throughout life, but are these needs best met in family life or elsewhere? (A fuller account of the subject of human needs can be found in *Skills for Caring – Clients as Individuals* and *Skills for Caring – Human Development*.)

PERSONAL NEEDS

Certain needs are universal to all human beings, for example the need for:

- **adequate food and drink**
- **shelter and physical comfort**
- **health care**
- **personal freedom.**

Physical needs, such as the need for food and shelter, are obvious, but emotional needs are more complicated. Some emotional needs are:

SECURITY

People have a life-long need to build a place which is safe and secure from any outside threat, whether the threat is physical or emotional. If they feel secure in their innermost selves they are able to face outside pressures and uncertainties. If people *don't* feel secure they are more likely to find it difficult to cope with forces outside their control.

GIVING AND RECEIVING AFFECTION

Most people prefer to live in relation to other people because they need to give and receive personal affection. This need becomes most apparent when it is not being met. Have you ever heard someone say, 'I've so much love to give – if only I had someone to give it to'?

Being intimate with someone is part of a person's need to feel secure and safe; the danger of intimacy is that one partner may dominate the relationship, preventing the other from expressing his or her personality fully.

FEELING DEPENDENT AND INDEPENDENT

People depend on others for a whole range of emotions and experiences, but they also need to know that there are people who depend on them. People need to have experience of living as separate, independent individuals too. Everyone needs to have a part of themselves which is entirely private – a space which is not entered even by the people closest to them.

Now try Exercise 9.

• •

EXERCISE 9

What is happening to your own needs?
• Which ones are being fulfilled?
• How are they being fulfilled?
• Which ones are not being fulfilled?
• How might they be fulfilled?

• •

We expect many of our personal needs to be met through family life, yet the behaviour occurring in families often runs counter to meeting these needs. Perhaps part of the problem is that we have an idealised view of family life which we think we should live up to. The myth of a 'perfect' family is encouraged by the manufacturers of products like soap powder or cereal who use it in advertisements to sell their products.

Also, if we believe in the idea of the family as the 'foundation of society' – a unit which binds society together and hands on valued beliefs – it can be difficult for us to come to terms with our own 'less-than-ideal' family.

Think about this further in Exercise 10.

• •

EXERCISE 10

What is 'less than ideal' in your family? Feel free to write down what you really think – no one will see your notes without your permission. Remember, it is important for you to have a thoughtful understanding of your own experience of family life.

• •

FAMILY EXPERIENCES

Our personalities are formed as we grow into adults. We may not be aware of it happening, but the nature of our personalities depends to a large extent on how we are able to express our needs. Our needs cannot be met in full – everyone has something missing from their lives. We are all 'damaged' in one way or another because of a lack of response to our needs at various stages of our lives. This damage is revealed when people use phrases like:

'I missed out as a child.'

'I never really had a chance to be an adolescent.'

'I was so much under the control of my parents that I was never able to be myself.'

If we feel we have 'missed out' during the various stages of growing up this may be directly connected with our experience of being in our family. Life in a family can be both rewarding and disturbing.

SUPPRESSION AND REPRESSION

If our experience of family life does not match the idealised picture we have, we may feel embarrassed or ashamed. What do we do with these experiences? We drive them underground. We find ways of compensating for the less-than-happy experiences in our own families by pretending that they do not exist. For example, we push down inside ourselves angry feelings about our parents. We have been taught not be angry with our parents because parents are supposed to know best. But this anger will not always remain silent – every now and then it surfaces and we are forced to admit it exists. What do we do? Do we let it out or push it back down again?

The word used to describe the process of shutting out different feelings is **'suppression'**. When we suppress our feelings we are trying to push them away from us because they are too

---

EXAMPLE

When a social worker had to deal with a child who had been abused she suddenly realised that she herself had been abused as a child. Soon all the memories of what had happened came flooding back. The social worker was taken completely by surprise because she had dealt with the abuse by putting it right out of her mind. Only when faced with another abused child was the social worker reminded of her own experience and her defence of apparently forgetting the disturbing experience evaporated.

difficult to acknowledge and talk about. But we know these feelings are there because they keep on disturbing us.

There are some feelings or experiences which are so powerful and painful that we *have* to shut them out of our memory – we cannot deal with them. We try to convince ourselves that these events didn't happen. We drive them deep into our subconscious and believe that we have forgotten them. This is called **'repression'**.

Both suppression and repression involve pushing away painful experiences and feelings. The difference is that we are aware of our suppressed feelings, but we are *not* aware of repressed feelings because we shut them away so firmly that we no longer think they exist. An example of the effects of repression is shown in the panel on page 10.
See Exercise 11.

● ●

EXERCISE 11

It is easy to find examples of suppression. Think about any angry feelings you have had which you find difficult to talk about. Perhaps you are frightened that if you do put your anger into words you may hurt other people, especially people you love. Fear of the destructive power of anger can sap your energy. Also, you may spend so much time trying not to hurt others you may feel that no one is paying attention to your needs.

Try to write down some of these examples and reflect on them in private.

● ●

It is important to know about both suppression and repression, but it is unlikely that you will be asked to deal with repression among clients. Working with people who have repressed past experiences requires highly specialised knowledge and training, something we cannot cover in this book. Suppressed feelings, on the other hand, are part of people's lives and you are likely to have to deal with them at some time.

FAMILY SECRETS

All families have secrets. Some secrets are known by members of the family but are not spoken about. Other secrets may be known by some members of the family but not by others. Those who know the secret anxiously try to keep it from those who don't; those who *don't* know sense there is

something wrong and want to find out what is going on! This creates a great deal of tension within the family.

If, for example, a family member has feelings which the rest of the family disapprove of, what does he do?
• Does he run away?
• Does he 'take on' the family and risk a fight?
• Does he set aside his own feelings and pretend that everying is all right?
• Does he try to talk to other members of the family?
See Exercise 12.

● ●

EXERCISE 12

What are the 'forbidden feelings' within your own family?
• Who has them?
• How are these feelings dealt with?
• How could the methods used to deal with these feelings be improved?
• What is your position, regarding this situation?

● ●

THE LOVE/HATE RELATIONSHIP

Clearly, powerful emotions – both positive and negative – take place within family life. This can result in people carrying around opposite feelings about themselves and those closest to them. They both love and hate themselves, and love and hate their family. The theory of object relations may help you understand this complex situation.

THE THEORY OF OBJECT RELATIONS

This theory is based on the idea that a baby at first sees things in 'black and white'. Either he gets what he wants ('good') or he doesn't get what he wants ('bad'). The baby sees the world as either good or bad. He divides everything around him – people and things – into 'good' or 'bad' objects.

Do you think that this theory applies to some of the situations that occur in a family? For example, when our parents are fighting we tend to support one more than the other – we 'take sides'. One parent seems to become the object of all the good things in our life and the other represents all the bad things in our life. Imagine a situation where a child sees her parents squabbling all the time. She finds herself taking her father's side – he can do no

© CHURCHILL LIVINGSTONE 1992 (COPYING BY PERMISSION ONLY)

wrong. On the other hand the child thinks her mother as always nagging, punishing and complaining. The child thinks that her mother never pays her any attention; it doesn't make any difference to her that her father is never around when he is needed.

The object relations theory suggests that we can hold opposite, and seemingly contradictory, views about ourselves and those close to us at the same time. You may find this idea puzzling, but *Exercise 13* may help you understand it better.

EXERCISE 13

The theory of object relations suggests that you 'relate' to certain 'objects' (or people) in certain ways. For you, a 'good' object may have been a teddy bear or blanket; a 'bad' object is something you hated.
Try to think of:
• objects you loved
• objects you hated
• 'people' objects you loved
• 'people' objects you hated.

SEX

Sex is not an easy subject to discuss because people often find it embarrassing. It is a part of life, but we pretend that it is not! Care workers have to come to terms with their own attitudes towards sex because they will be working with other people's attitudes.

Care workers' attitudes should not interfere with their clients' lives. For example, an intimate relationship between two people in a residential home for elderly people is often frowned upon or ridiculed. It is disturbing to think of two elderly people being forced to find a secret corner to meet together, on their own, away from disapproving or joking glances. It would be unfair only to blame care workers for such a situation. Often, the children of a resident become so upset that their parent is involved in an intimate relationship with another resident that they will try to persuade the staff not to allow the relationship to continue. In doing this, they are forgetting that if we diminish (reduce) a person's sexual self we also diminish a basic part of his own being.

Look at your own attitudes to sex and sexuality by working on an extended exercise, Exercise 14.

EXERCISE 14

This extended exercise will give you an opportunity to work out some of your own attitudes about sex. It will also help you to gain a better understanding of the way other people view sexuality.

NOTE: This is a private exercise and you will not be asked to show what you have written to anyone else. Because it is private, try to be as honest with yourself as possible. There aren't any 'right' or 'wrong' answers. Your answers will reveal something about your attitude to sex and sexuality and, as you go over them, they will help you understand clearly what your own views are. You will find this helpful when you work with your clients', and their families', attitudes to sex.

1   How old were you when you first found out the 'facts of life'?
2   How did you find out and who told you?
3   Were your parents involved in helping you find out?
    • If 'Yes' – were you pleased or embarrassed?
      – what was it like, having parents tell you?
    • If 'No' – would you have liked parents to have told you?
      – what do you feel about them *not* having told you?
4   Do you, or did you, masturbate?
    • If 'Yes' – what are your feelings about masturbation? Are they feelings of: dirtiness/ guilt/frustration/anger/relief/ pleasure/fulfilment/any other?
      – if you feel guilt rather than pleasure, why do you think this is (especially if it is true that most people masturbate)?
    • If 'No' – why do you think this is, when so many other people masturbate?
5   Think about your first sexual experience with another person. It doesn't have to have been sexual intercourse, but it does have to have been sexual. How would you describe it?
    • Did it colour your feelings about any later sexual experiences?
    • In what way?

6 If you have not had an actual sexual relationship with another person:
   • Why do you think this is?
   • What do you feel about not having had such an experience?

7 What is your view about people who live together in a sexual relationship without being married?

8 Children are normally born as a result of a man and a woman having intercourse, but they grow up in a wide variety of settings. As part of a:
   • family with a husband and wife
   • family where the parents are not married
   • single parent family
   • family where the adults are in a lesbian or homosexual relationship with one another
   • group rather than a family, such as a group care home.
   With specific reference to sex and sexuality, what are your views and feelings about children growing up in these settings? Use one or two words to describe each setting.

9 Have you previously had sex with other people other than your spouse or partner, or only with your spouse or partner? Whatever your answer, identify those adjectives listed which describe your feelings about this situation. Add some more words, if you wish.
   Nothing at all/pleased with yourself/ frustrated/angry/fulfilled/guilty/ unfulfilled/left out/relieved/vulnerable/ scared/other feelings.

10 Have you had sex outside your marriage or partnership? Whether you answer 'Yes' or 'No' what are your feelings about it?
   Nothing at all/pleased with yourself/ frustrated/angry/fulfilled/guilty/ unfulfilled/left out/relieved/vulnerable/ scared/other feelings.

11 Have you had a sexual experience – not necessarily sexual intercourse, but definitely sexual – with someone of your own gender?
   • Whatever your answer, 'Yes' or 'No' what do you feel about it?
   • What do you feel about people who have lesbian or homosexual relationships, or about people who have both heterosexual and homosexual relations?

12 What do you think about your parents having sex?

13 What do you think about your unmarried children over 16 having sex?

14 What are your thoughts about AIDS?
   • Who do you think are the most likely people to get AIDS?
   • Do you know anyone who has AIDS or who is HIV positive?
   • Do you think you might be at risk from infection, either through your sexual behaviour or through your partner's sexual behaviour?
   • What is your view of people you consider are at risk from the infection?

15 What are your views about contraception?

16 What are your views about abortion?

17 This question is about fathers, uncles, daughters and nieces. Answer 'Yes', 'No' or 'Depends' to the following statements. If you answer 'Depends' say on what your answer depends.
   • A daughter should be encouraged to climb up onto her father's knee.
   • A niece should be encouraged to climb up onto her uncle's knee, even if she seems a little shy about doing so.
   • It is harmless fun if an uncle tickles his niece.
   • A daughter should not be allowed to climb into her parents' bed while they are in it.
   • A daughter should be allowed to climb into her parent's bed when only her father is in bed.
   • A father should bath and dry his daughter as long as she needs to be bathed and dried.
   • The bathroom door should remain unlocked as far as family members are concerned. A father and daughter should have no objection to seeing each other without any clothes on.
   • Unless either father or daughter prefers not to, there is nothing wrong with a father and his adult daughter seeing each other without any clothes on.
   • A father and daughter should be able to talk to each other about sex. (continued)

- A father should be able to cuddle his daughter, up to the age of 10 years, without worrying what parts of their bodies come into contact with each other.
- From the time she is a baby, a father should exercise extreme caution about touching his daughter.
- An uncle and niece should be able to cuddle each other as intimately as a father and a daughter.

18 This question is about mothers, sons, aunts and nephews. The relationship between male adults and female children has been given a lot of attention, but what about that between female adults and male children? Think about the following views and note your thoughts in writiing, if you wish.
- It is often assumed that male sexuality is more demanding and intrusive than female sexuality. Is this true?
- Is women's sexuality only passive?
- What happens to a women's sexuality as she watches her son growing into an independent young man?
- How does a mother relate to her grown up son?

19 This question is about sex and older people. As before, answer 'Yes', 'No' or 'Depends' then say on what your answer depends.
- Older people don't look sexy or appear interested in sex.
- Older people who are being intimate in the presence of others are embarrassing.
- Older people's sex lives can be as exciting as younger people's.
- Older people should be encouraged to slow down, or even stop, their sex lives because it is bad for their health.
- Older people who develop a new relationship should be given every opportunity to convert their relationship into an active sexual one, if they wish.
- Where necessary, older people should be helped physically by another adult to have sex together.
- What do you think about this statement: 'Older people actually having sexual intercourse is a bit distasteful – too much emphasis is placed on it'?

20 The final question is about sex and people with physical disabilities or learning difficulties. ('Learning difficulties' is the term which has replaced 'mental handicap'.) As before, answer 'Yes', 'No' or 'Depends' and if you answer 'Depends' then say on what your answer depends.
- Physically disabled people and those with learning difficulties have exactly the same personal needs as the rest of us, and one of those needs is for sex.
- People with a learning difficulty should not be encouraged to develop intimate personal relations which may lead to sex because this will create problems for other people.
- A physically disabled couple who are attracted to each other should, if necessary, be helped by someone else to achieve sexual intercourse together.
- Helping a physically disabled couple to achieve sexual intercourse is wrong because their level of dependence and disability prevents them from doing something which is essentially a private matter. If they are unable to do it for themselves then they need to come to terms with the physical limitations of their relationship.
- The sexual drives of people with a learning difficulty should be played down rather than encouraged because they are not able to make informed choices about how to give expression to their sexuality.
- A hostel for young adults with a learning difficulty should not provide sex education and should discourage any sexual activity.
- The parents' views on sexuality in relation to a son or daughter with a learning difficulty should be respected, even if their view denies their child one of a person's basic needs.
- A programme of sex education should be introduced into a hostel for young adults with a learning difficulty because they will be experiencing internal sexual drives and frustrations like anyone else.)

We could probably continue Exercise 14 for a whole chapter! You could always add further questions of your own about sexual attitudes, if you wish. You might also find it helpful to read *Skills for Caring – Independent Living* which considers in greater detail our attitudes to people with a disability and the effect they have on the lives of disabled people.

If you have answered the questions and commented on the statements honestly you should be able to put together a picture of your own attitudes to the complex subject of human sexual behaviour. Perhaps you found some of the questions surprising at first, but as you worked through each one you probably became more comfortable with the subject. If *you* feel comfortable about the subject of sex it will be easier for you to work with clients whose situation involves discussing sex, especially if the clients themselves are feeling awkward about the topic.

THE ARRIVAL OF A BABY

A baby can bring feelings of supreme joy *and* near terror to a family! A couple feel joy when they think, 'How could the two of us have created such a beautiful, perfect new being?' and terror when they wonder, 'What have we let ourselves in for? Is it going to be like this for the rest of our lives?' This section on the effect a baby has on a family assumes that the baby is born healthy, following a normal delivery, to a couple who are in a stable relationship. Obviously, if the baby is born damaged, the mother is on her own, or the family is in severe poverty there will be additional problems which we cannot look into in this short text.

JOYS AND WORRIES

The front of a baby's head is soft; the rest of him is smooth and downy and he has a very special scent. When an adult strokes, sniffs and kisses a baby's head it shows there is complete trust and protection between adult and baby. Also, a baby's face is so elastic it reveals everything about how he is feeling; this arouses strong emotions in a parent. A baby's first smile shows that he recognises his parent and that a relationship is forming. If you have an experience of babies you will have many more examples of your own about the way adults react to a baby.

However, there is another side to the joy and wonder people feel about a baby, as the statements in the next exercise show.

See Exercise 15.

• •

EXERCISE 15

What scenes do the following statements bring to mind? Do they sound true to life?

• 'Today I found myself crying into a bucket of nappies.'
• 'I can't even find time to wash my own hair.'
• 'Why is my mother always feeding the baby while I'm washing the nappies?'
• 'Once, when I was staying with my aunt, I had to get up in the middle of the night to change and feed the baby. Suddenly and quietly she appeared, brought me a cup of tea, took away and washed the dirty nappy, and allowed me just to sit with my baby. What bliss!'
• 'Why does my mother-in-law constantly tell me what to do in a way that makes me feel stupid and incompetent? I would really value her advice if only she would give it in a way which didn't put me down.'
• 'How am I going to assure my elder child that my love for him has not lessened as a result of the arrival of his baby sister?'
• 'Why is my friend's baby starting to use a cup, but I can't get mine away from the bottle?'
• 'She's just sicked up her medicine again. What will I do? Phone the doctor *again*?'
• 'Why is my husband behaving like a baby? Is he jealous?'
• 'Make love? I'm so tired – I must try and get some sleep before the baby cries again.'
• 'I need him to look after me while we are both looking after the baby. I know he needs me and I can respond to that as long as he doesn't give the impression that has to compete with the baby for my affection.'
• 'Why am I repeating jobs endlessly all day long? As soon as I finish a job it has to be done again.'

Perhaps you could add some other scenes of your own?

• •

© CHURCHILL LIVINGSTONE 1992 (COPYING BY PERMISSION ONLY)

Exercise 15 should make you aware of the enormous amount of work involved in looking after a baby and the feelings of exhaustion which can sometimes overcome a new parent (even when the baby is healthy and the couple are in a stable relationship). A whole range of new emotions affect all members of the family, in different ways. Although the questions in Exercise 15 were put from the mother's point of view some of them refer to what other members of the family could be thinking.

BONDING

While the family comes to terms with this new range of emotions a vitally important experience is taking place between the baby and (usually) his mother. This powerful connection is known as **bonding**. The experience of bonding helps the parent cope with the hardships suggested in Exercise 15.

Sometimes the act of bonding does not come easily. If it does not come as strongly or readily as would have been expected this has a profound effect on the baby's mother.

'Baby blues'

'Baby blues' describes the situation where a mother is finding it hard to cope with the demanding and exhausting times she is having with her baby. She regularly bursts into tears without warning; she is desperate for someone to take the baby away and give her some peace; and she is frightened that she is not capable of looking after him. This situation is not uncommon – very few mothers do not experience these feelings from time to time. 'Baby blues' should be accepted as a natural reaction, although during these periods a mother needs a lot of extra help.

Post-natal depression

Although some of the signs of 'baby blues' appear in **post-natal depression** the two conditions are quite different. If a mother goes into post-natal depression she has almost given up and can hardly do anything for her baby. She is unmoved by his demanding cries and uninterested in showing him love. A mother in this situation is ill and needs professional help and treatment.

FAMILY HISTORY REPEATED

Some families repeat their way of life one generation after another. For example, perhaps a father who worked as a miner vows, 'I'll make sure no son of mine ever has to go down the pits'. Yet the son probably becomes a miner because of reasons outside the family's control, such as a lack

EXAMPLES

- Physical punishment – Have you ever heard someone say, 'I was given the belt at school, and by my father, and it never did me any harm'? This is a common excuse given by parents who are being asked to consider whether they may be treating their children too severely.

- Child abuse – Many parents who abuse their children were abused themselves as children. Almost without being aware of it parents remember how they were brought up and, even in cases where they suffered at the hands of their parents, they do the same thing with their own children. Perhaps you think the opposite would occur, but it could be that the way *their* parents behaved towards children is stamped so heavily on the memory of abusing parents that they know no other way to behave when they themselves become parents.

- Incest – Incest is a severe form of child abuse. As with the behaviour of a parent involved in child abuse, you would expect that, for example, a mother who had been the victim of incest in her own family would make sure that her own daughter is not abused. However, when incest is discovered in a family it is often revealed that incest also took place between members of the mother's or father's family.

> INCEST: SEXUAL INTERCOURSE BETWEEN PEOPLE (FOR EXAMPLE, BROTHER AND SISTER) SO CLOSELY RELATED THAT THEY ARE FORBIDDEN BY LAW TO MARRY.

of alternative employment in the area. Or a parent says, 'I want to give my children what I never had myself' yet treats his children in exactly the same way as *he* was treated by *his* parents.

Patterns of behaviour can be carried on from one generation to another. Sometimes these patterns of behaviour are unacceptable, as the examples given on page 16 show.

The examples given are only brief descriptions of family history repeating itself. They are not intended to address the complex nature of child abuse in families, a subject which is covered in detail in *Skills for Caring - Protecting Children and Young People*.

Complete this chapter by trying Exercise 16.

● ●

EXERCISE 16

Take some time to think of ways in which history has repeated itself through generations of your own family:

● What parts of the family history are you proud of?
● What parts make you feel uncomfortable?
● Is there anything in your family history which you think is being repeated but which is being kept secret?

● ●

Further information about the various stages of life can be found in *Skills for Caring – Human Development*.

In Chapter 3 we will look at the different ways care workers can work with families.

3
Working with families

■ The complexities of family life can appear quite daunting to care workers. This chapter explores different ways of working with families and discusses those which you, as care workers, may find helpful. It also looks at ways of working which you should avoid because they are *not* helpful for your clients.

There are lots of ways of living a family life.

EXAMPLES

- Bedtimes – You may wonder why the children in a client's family are up so late when in *your* family they would be out of the way much earlier. Perhaps having a child curled up on the couch wrapped in a blanket is as loving a gesture as tucking it up in a bed with a story at 7 p.m.?
- Attitudes – You may be shocked to see the children doing what they like when you are used to keeping children under stricter control. Or you may be concerned about children who are so well behaved that they seem unable to decide for themselves what they want to do.
- Presents – you may be appalled that parents who struggle to make ends meet spend so much on Christmas presents for their children, leaving them to cope with the debts from their spending for the rest of the year. You may think the parents are buying affection, but this may be their way of showing how much they value their children.

Many of the ways you will come across in other families will be very different from your own. You must be careful not to judge other families, or be critical of them, because they do not do things in the way you would. Some examples of differences between families are described in the panel.

When you have looked at the examples, try Exercise 17.

EXERCISE 17

- Think of 2 families whose attitudes and way of life are very different from those of your own family. Make a short list of your own family's attitudes.
- When you have done this, make a short list of what you feel to be the key differences between these 2 families and your own.
- Finally, go through your lists and try to identify *why* these differences exist.

Exercise 17 should help you recognise that families do have different attitudes and do behave in different ways, often for very good reasons. When you work with families consider what their reasons might be for the way they do things.

BEGIN WHERE PEOPLE ARE

When you start working with a family you cannot assume that both you and the family know what the issues are. You may have one idea; the family may have another. The family may be quite suspicious of the reasons why you are there. You have to give the family opportunities to tell you why they think you are there and what they think the problems are.

EXAMPLE

Lizzie is a care worker in a hostel for young people who have been discharged from a psychiatric hospital but who are not yet ready to go back home. The parents of a young man who stays in the hostel come to visit and a family meeting is held. Lizzie is keen to persuade the parents to let their son return home because both she and the hostel team think he is ready to leave. The parents are very nervous about this idea because they have many other problems to deal with, including the fact that the husband may be made redundant. They also suspect that the hostel just want to get rid of their son by sending him back to them. Lizzie feels frustrated because the unit's policy is to return people to the community as soon as possible.

In this situation, although Lizzie believes that it is right for the son to return home she may not have any understanding of the parents' position and the many other worries on their minds. Before Lizzie suggests anything she should find out more about the parents' point of view. Perhaps they are simply worried about whether they will be able to look after their son by themselves.

If their understanding of the problems is different from yours you cannot simply brush them aside and get on with what *you* think they should be doing. You must take the family's understanding into account and work from there, as the example on the left shows.

Think about this further in Exercise 18.

EXERCISE 18

Think of an occasion, either in your own family or in someone else's when you felt that the family was being intruded upon by another person, someone who seemed to be trying to get the family to do or think something against the family's own wishes.
- **How did this situation arise?**
- **Why was the family uncomfortable with what was happening?**
- **What would have been a better way of going about things?**

HELP THE FAMILY TO HELP THEMSELVES

When you and the family you are working with have had time to feel comfortable with one another, you can start to build up a picture of the issues and problem areas the family is dealing with. Often, you will sympathize with the family in the difficulties they are facing, but you must not be tempted to try and be helpful too quickly. It is important to give the members of the family a chance to work things out for themselves. Be patient in encouraging them to explore the various courses of action available to them and then help them to make up their own minds about what to do. The example below shows how this can work in practice.

Now try Exercise 19.

EXAMPLE

Joe works in a hostel for physically disabled adults. Recently, the parents of one young man living in the hostel discovered that he had formed an attraction for one of the female residents. As far as Joe was concerned this was all right, but the young man's parents were appalled. They could not accept that severely disabled people could be attracted to one another.

Joe knew that, when he discussed the situation with the parents, he could easily make statements like, 'Of course it's all right for them to fancy each other.' He also knew that he could probably persuade the parents that he was right. However, he decided not to take this approach because it would not give the parents the opportunity to think through their position. They needed to come to their own conclusion about their son's attraction to someone who was, after all, *another* family's daughter.

EXAMPLE

A home help suggested to an elderly client that she might allow her 38-year-old daughter, who had Down's Syndrome, to go to the shops with her (the home help) one day. No date was fixed so that the home help could take a week or two to help her elderly client adjust to this new idea. She did this by following a step-by-step strategy:

- Every now and then the home help mentioned the idea of an outing to her elderly client, but she was careful to approach the subject sensitively.
- Eventually, the mother accepted the idea although she was very anxious about it.
- The idea was openly talked about in a planned and controlled way, between daughter, mother and home help, as something which was definitely going to happen.
- The home help and the daughter made detailed preparations for the outing the day before it was due. For example, they prepared the shopping list and told the mother exactly where they would be going.

The home help and the young woman went on the outing, told the mother all about it on their return, and repeated the process several times over the next few weeks. They always bought the same range of goods, spent the same amount of money and checked the change.

Once the elderly mother had accepted her daughter's ability to go on a shopping trip, the home help went out with the daughter again but this time walked at a distance behind her. She kept an eye on her but let *her* do the shopping. After the daughter and the home help had followed this routine a few times, the mother was reassured that her daughter could manange and allowed her to go out alone.

EXERCISE 19

Imagine a situation where you are very concerned about the well-being of a close friend. Your friend's family are going through a troubled time and you are upset to see how much this is distressing your friend. You think you know what needs to be done so you tell the family what you think is the solution to their difficulties. However, you soon become impatient with the family's apparent inability to see things your way. Perhaps you can think of an occasion when you *actually* behaved in this way. Think about this for a few minutes then try to answer the following questions:

- Why would you feel impatient because this family could not see your point of view?
- What might be stopping the family from seeing things your way?
- Did you express you views too quickly?
  - If so, what effect would this have on the family?
  - If not, why was it the right time to contribute?

TAKE CHANGE ONE STEP AT A TIME

In some situations you may find that members of the family are not able to find out for themselves what needs to be changed in their pattern of family life and you may have to be more active in suggesting changes. Do not suggest a whole range of ideas which the family may be unable to accept all at once. It is better to go one stage at a time and support the family at each stage. Do not go on to the next stage until the family feels comfortable with the first stage. The example on the left illustrates the step-by-step approach.

The home help succeeded with her suggestion because she took one step at a time and prepared both her clients for change. If she had done nothing except tell the mother, 'I'm sending your daughter out alone' her elderly client would probably have refused to consider such a shocking idea. Because the home help discussed everything involved at each stage the mother had time to adjust to the changes.

See Exercise 20.

EXERCISE 20

Imagine that you work as a care worker in a residential school which normally allows the young people to return home to their families at weekends. You notice that a particular boy has been making a number of half-hearted excuses for staying at the school rather than going home. You discover that the reason is the constant fighting that takes place between father and son because the father drinks heavily at weekends. Set out a plan which clearly outlines the steps you would need to take to bring this situation out into the open so that it could be discussed.

AVOID TAKING OVER

Take care that you do not appear to be the one who can do what another family member cannot do, especially whre children are involved. For example, a health visitor found a distraught mother trying to soothe her screaming baby. The health visitor picked up the baby who became quiet. Delighted that she had been the one to calm the baby the health visitor suggested that *she*, and not the mother, continue the feeding which had caused the screaming. Although the mother resented this she handed over the plate and spoon. The health visitor confidently started feeding the child who was promptly sick all over her. She was taught a lesson, but the mother was left feeling confused and less confident.

Try Exercise 21.

EXERCISE 21

Think of a time as a mother, father, son or daughter you have felt that someone else had taken over a part of your life.

- What was that person trying to do to you?
- What was your reaction?
- Why was the other person behaving in such a way?
- What was it about you that seemed to be prompting the other person to behave towards you in this way?

THE PERFECT WORKER

You must also be aware of the temptation to be the perfect worker. As your work with the family begins to succeed, and you are seen as someone useful, the family may think you are the solution to all their problems. You must resist this idea because you will not be doing the family a service

EXAMPLE

A student on a caring course was given a placement in a psychiatric hospital. The hospital believed it was important to work with people in the community, in their own homes. This work was usually carried out by staff working in pairs.

The student was therefore asked to join a member of staff, in this case of the opposite sex, to visit the home of a young married couple. The husband had recently been discharged from the hospital, but the couple were still finding it difficult to communicate with one another.

From the start, the student and her colleague got on well with the young couple. The young couple admired the way they were able to talk to each other, and the student and her colleague enjoyed the esteem the couple showed towards them.

Soon, the four of them were getting on so well that they agreed to swap positions. The student and her colleague played the part of husband and wife and the couple listened and reacted to them. The exercise was a success because the couple could see clearly how they were behaving towards one another and took new steps to sort things out.

The student and her colleague were pleased that they had been useful to the couple. However, if they had left the couple with the idea that they could live successfully only through them then the joy the couple felt at rediscovering one another would have disappeared as soon as the meetings finished.

if they become so dependent on you that they cannot do much for themselves.

Instead, always encourage families to do what they are able and make sure that the course of action you are encouraging a family to take is one the members can continue when you have stopped working with them.

However, it is important that you feel useful to the family – that is the rewarding part of the work for you. The family will put their trust in you and you have to use that trust to help them through the various stages of their difficulties. The example on page 21 shows how this can be done.

Now try Exercise 22.

● ●

EXERCISE 22

Think of a time when you or your family placed a great deal of trust in someone outside your family. Or think of a time when another family put their trust in you, and treated you as the one person who could sort out their problems.

- Briefly write down what happened for either situation.
- What was the nature of the trust the family put in the other person?
- Was it justified?
- How did the other person handle being made to feel so important?

● ●

RECEIVING CONFIDENCES

Gradually, you and the family you are working with will become more comfortable and confident with one another. When this happens, members of the family may tell you things that they would not tell either each other or their best friends. This puts you in a very privileged position. You are someone to whom it is safe to talk because you are not a member of the family (so you will not over-react to what you are told) and because you are trusted. You must treat your position of trust with respect.

When a member of the family gives you some information in confidence, ask yourself these questions:

- **Why is he telling me this – there must be a reason?**
- **What does he want me to do with the information?**

- **Does he want me to help him find a way to tell the person he should be telling?**
- **Does he want me to do the telling for him?**

If you discuss these questions with the person you will be able to come to an agreement about what to do with the information he has given you. Although there are exceptions, in most cases you should not do anything with this information until you have reached such an agreement.

See Exercise 23.

● ●

EXERCISE 23

A teenage girl you know quite well has told you she is pregnant. She is frightened of telling her parents but has confided in you because you are a care worker and she trusts you. The girl is desperate to talk to someone about her situation. Some of her worries are:

- She is doing well at school and wants to go to college.
- She thinks her parents would be so appalled at the news of her pregnancy that they would not want to have anything more to do with her.
- She has a serious relationship with her boyfriend but has not yet told him of the pregnancy.
- She feels that she would be able to speak more easily to her boyfriend's parents than to her own.
- She is scared at the thought of making choices about abortion, adoption or keeping the baby.

You would probably be pleased that the girl has felt able to talk to you but feel anxious about the responsibility it involves. Write down what things you might do and the order in which you would do them.

You will find more information on the subject of confidentiality on page 25.

● ●

SELF-DISCLOSURE

A care worker may choose to share her own family experience with the family she is working with, in the hope that it will increase the family's understanding of their situation. The term for this method of sharing experience is **self-disclosure**.

When you are telling a family something about yourself try to avoid 2 extremes. The first extreme occurs when what is happening in this family also happened in your own. It is tempting to talk about your experience, explain how members of your family solved their problems and then say 'You do the same'. You must resist this temptation because you cannot assume that something which worked for your family would work in the same way for another family. The second extreme is saying nothing at all about yourself. This is not helpful either, because it can be comforting for your clients to know that you are able to understand some of the troubles they are going through from your own experience.

Try to find a middle way between the 2 extremes of self-disclosure. You want to reach out towards the family and show them that you are human too. If you tell them about your experience of a similar situation it can make them feel less despondent about theirs. You also want to share in their joy when they achieve something.

If you are unsure about when to share personal experiences, remember that you should only do so if you think it would be helpful for your clients. You should not be talking about your own family only because you want the clients to listen to some of your problems.

See Exercise 24.

COPING WITH DIFFICULT FEELINGS

As you gain the confidence of the family, you may find that you are listening to an increasing amount of disturbing material. Members of the family may find great relief in talking to you, but you may find it difficult to cope with the painful experiences they are sharing with you.

For example, Usha is a care worker who works with families who have pre-school children with severe and profound learning difficulties. The children were either born with learning difficulties or were involved in a serious accident. Every family Usha visits is working through a personal tragedy. Her job is to help other members of the family come to terms with what has happened. She has to help them to live and grow through their pain so that the child with the learning difficulty will feel loved and secure.

The families are grateful for Usha's interest and regular visiting because it gives them an opportunity to share their fears and feelings. What the families do not realise is the effect this has on Usha, who feels that she is moving from one tragedy to the next throughout her working day. She comes home to her own family exhausted and depressed, and has very little energy left to enjoy her own family or to meet their, or her own, needs.

EXERCISE 24

Perhaps one of your clients is a mother who has just been told that she has breast cancer. The lady's family is very upset, but they do not know that you too have had breast cancer. You have recently completed a course of chemotherapy following a lumpectomy.

You can see that the family is deeply distressed as they think of all the worst things that could happen. You have recently been told by the specialist that, as far as he can judge, all the cancer has been removed and you only need to visit him every 3 months.

What do you tell the family about your circumstances?

- Do you tell them everything and say that you are sure their mother will make a good recovery, too?
- Do you decide not to tell them anything?
- You have not had the time, or an opportunity, to talk about your own feelings with anyone. Do you start talking about your own worries with your clients?
- Do you tell them that you know something about what they are going through because you and your family have been through it as well?
- What else might you do or say?

Write down two brief lists. One list should be the kind of things you think would be appropriate to tell the family about your own experience; the other should be a list of the things that would be unhelpful for the family to know about your own experience.

It is very important that you have regular supervision when you are involved in this kind of work. During supervision sessions you should be given the opportunity to talk about any discomfort you feel with the experiences the family are sharing with you. If you do not have an outlet to express these feelings, there is a possibility that you will avoid dealing with them by seeing them as something that the family, but not *you*, has to work through.

BEING GENEROUS TOWARDS OTHER CARE WORKERS

You may not be the only care worker who is involved with the family. If so, you must be careful not to undermine the work of other care workers or get into competition with them. Although this may seem obvious, it is very easy to become possessive towards the family you are working with and to find that you are unwilling to admit that other people may also be carrying out good work with them.

You may have experienced a situation like the following one: A multi-disciplinary case conference was held in a residential centre for people who have a mental illness. It was attended by various people – a psychiatrist, a social worker, a psychologist, and a main grade care worker who was the key worker to the person who was going to be discussed. As the discussion developed, the care worker noticed that before people made a comment they would make remarks such as 'I don't know this family all that well, but . . .' or 'I am sure there are others who know more about this situation than I, but . . .'

The care worker realised that these people were competing with each other. They were trying to show who knew most about the family, and whose ideas for the family were best. Gradually, the care worker understood that the family was being used as a battleground where professional rivalries were being fought out.

See Exercise 25.

• •

EXERCISE 25

The following exercise is about a health visitor who visits a family with a young child. Her main concern is the well-being and growth of the baby, but she has noticed that the family is in some distress because of their poverty and the young couple's inability to manage their home life. The health visitor also knows that a home carer from the social services department is involved with this family.

• How might the health visitor use this information? Make some notes of your ideas.

• •

No one would expect you to know exactly what to do in the situation described in Exercise 25, particularly if you are not working in a care situation. But Exercise 25 will help you consider what steps you *might* take to involve other care workers when the need of a family goes beyond your own job remit or area of skill.

BEING RELIABLE

The families you work with will probably have had a lot of experience of waiting for other people to provide them with the help they need. They may have waited for:

• **hospital appointments**
• **aids to help them with their disability**
• **adaptations to their house**
• **the health visitor to arrive**
• **their allowance book to be sorted out**
• **the social fund to come to their help**
• **hospital results**
• **the social worker to return at the time she promised**
• **answers to letters**
• **replies to complaints**
• **information about which school their child with special needs will be placed in.**

Almost all the waiting involved in these situations is associated with hardship or anxiety, which adds to the stress felt by the family.

Try Exercise 26.

- -

EXERCISE 26

Can you think of a time when you needed help from other people or from other agencies? Did you receive help promptly or did you have to wait? If you had to wait try to describe your experience and your feelings at the time.

- -

DEVELOPING CONFIDENCE

If you are working with a family in their own home you must train yourself to be sensitive to what is going on in the house as you enter. You may not be introduced to any other people who are there. If so, it is all right to ask, 'Is it all right for me to be here just now? Are you happy to talk at the moment?' Be prepared to leave if it is not a convenient time for you to call and always make absolutely sure that the family is willing for you to proceed.

For example, imagine you have arrived at a family's home, by prior appointment, to discuss a potentially delicate issue. You are warmly received, but as you go into the house you find strangers there. They happen to be neighbours. You know that you are there by prior arrangement and that the family has been expecting you, but the family do not make any moves to explain the presence of the neighbours and the neighbours do not attempt to get up and go. It seems that the family feel the next move is up to you because they have handed you the responsibility to decide what happens next. Unless you join in the pleasantries and wait for something to happen – risking a wasted visit –
you will have to take the initiative. You will have to address the family, confirm that you are here for a purpose and ask them if it is all right to start. You will then know whether:

- **The family are worried about the planned discussion and the neighbours are there so that it cannot take place.**
- **The family has already told the neighours something about the issue and want them to join in.**
- **The neighbours, realising this is a private meeting, will make moves to leave.**

ACCOUNTABILITY AND CONFIDENTIALITY

If you work with families you may at some time receive personal and confidential material. A family, and the individuals within it, are free to tell you whatever they want; it would not be appropriate for you to stop them on the basis that you cannot cope with what they are telling you.

However, it is your responsibility to listen carefully to what you are told and then work through the dilemma of what you are going to do with the information. We have already mentioned the importance of getting permission to take the information elsewhere (see page 22). It is also important that you let clients know at an early stage of your work with them, that you work in an agency or organisation. Make it clear that your normal procedure is to inform your supervisor about what happens in your work activities. If this is made clear to your clients you will find it easier to handle any dilemmas which involve confidential information.

The following guidelines are helpful when dealing with these situations:

- **You should never feel that you have to take personal responsibility for dealing with confidential information by yourself.**
- **You are not bound to absolute confidentiality in the way that, for example, a priest is when he is given information in the confessional.**
- **You should always be accountable (in most care settings) to somebody else for your work.**
- **If you consider that someone is at risk as a result of what you have been told you must act on what you have been told.**
- **If you think that you must act, you must also tell the person who gave you the information what action you are going to take and why you are taking it.**
- **Although you want to preserve the confidential nature of your work with people and families, you cannot be sworn to secrecy.**

When you are working through the difficulties of a dilemma involving confidential information it is comforting to remember that when someone tells you something confidential which may affect others, he is often doing so because he *wants* to find a way of letting the others know.

4

Groups – a systems approach

■ In some ways groups are like families, because there is so much going on between the individuals in groups that members of a group can experience many different feelings, including joy, fulfilment, amusement, bewilderment and dejection. The members of groups are not biologically linked like the members of families but they become linked together in other ways.

WHAT IS A GROUP?

People gathered together in one place do not form a group unless they are all involved in one task. For example, the people in a hospital ward, lunch club for elderly people or training centre for people with learning difficulties form one kind of group. They have not come together because they wanted to be with one another, but because they each needed or wanted to be in a particular place. However, if someone in the hospital ward or centre was taken ill then the people gathered there would have to do something about what had happened. In other words, they would have become a group with a task.

Similarly, if you are in a lift with a crowd of people you would not think that each of you was a member of a group. But if the lift became stuck between two floors then you and the other passengers would immediately become a group because you would all be working together to think of a way to get out.

In this chapter, the word 'group' will refer to 3 collections of people; those who:

- **are together because they just happen to be there**
- **are together but are not working on a task together**

- **are together specifically to work on a task together.**

Staff teams and management teams form groups as well as residents, day care attenders and patients. If you are doing a job with other people you are part of a group and need to know:

- **how your group operates**
- **the effects of group behaviour.**

THE SYSTEMS THEORY

> SYSTEM: AN ORGANISED WHOLE WITHIN WHICH THERE ARE A NUMBER OF SUB-SYSTEMS EACH WORKING IN RELATIONSHIP WITH ONE ANOTHER TO ACHIEVE A GOAL.

We use the word system to describe, for example, the organisation of traffic in a city. A traffic system is made up of logically interacting sub-systems, such as the underground system, bus system and train system. Each part of the system is planned and each part needs the other (see Figure 1).

There are 2 kinds of system – **closed** and **open**. A closed system is one in which the boundary around the system is impermeable, that is, nothing can get through. A closed system rejects all influences from the outside world. An open system has a permeable boundary, that is, it lets things through. It takes in influences from the outside and depends on them to function and grow. The system achieves its task by combining outside influences with what is already inside.

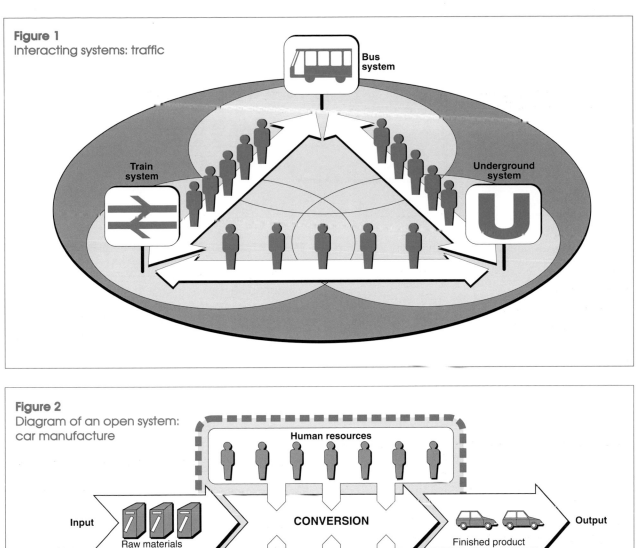

Figure 1
Interacting systems: traffic

Figure 2
Diagram of an open system:
car manufacture

Various terms are used to describe what happens in an open system:

- **input** – **influences and resources which the system needs from outside itself to do its job**
- **conversion** – **the combination of what is already inside the system (people, equipment, expertise) with what is brought into the system from outside**
- **output** – **the result of input and conversion, that is, what the system produces.**

For example, an organisation (or system) like a car manufacturing company imports raw materials (input) and combines them with equipment, resources and manpower (conversion) to produce cars (output) (see Figure 2).

We can apply the systems theory to human relations whether within caring organisations or as individual people. As individual people we are open systems. We take in material from outside ourselves, combine it with what is already within us and the output is our continuing growth.

However, open systems are poor containers of anxiety. If the outside world becomes too challenging or hostile we build a cocoon around ourselves and become a closed system. We say to ourselves, 'Enough is enough. I can't take much more. Leave me alone – I don't want to know.'

Depending on how comfortable we are about what is going on around us as we move backwards

Figure 3
Movement between systems

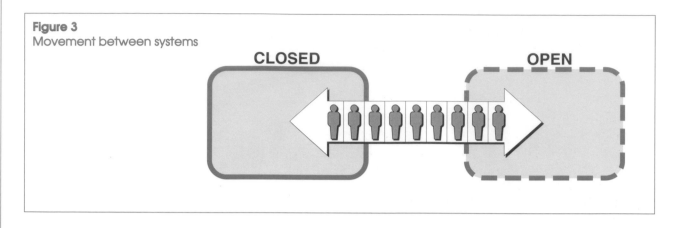

CLOSED **OPEN**

and forwards along a line between an open system and a closed system. Unless we are completely fixed in our views, we move along the line according to how prepared we are to work with issues outside us (see Figure 3). This also applies to the groups we work in and the way things happen in our workplace.

An example of this movement between systems is the situation which resulted from recommendations issued by the Second Vatican Council of the Roman Catholic Church in 1962. The recommendations suggested that monastic and religious life should become more open. The rigid rules which regulated, for example, life in a convent were to be relaxed so that the nuns communicated more freely with one another and with the outside world.

Although this move was welcomed, involvement in more relaxed relationships meant that nuns had to deal with new issues and conflicts and this caused great anxiety. Many nuns thought, 'This new way of going about our lives is all very well, but it is creating unhappiness. Things were safer in the old days'. The nuns were facing the difficulties of moving to and fro along the line of the new open system, which allowed fresh opportunities, and the old closed system, which was safe but avoided the complexities of living.

Try Exercise 27.

• •

EXERCISE 27

Think of yourself, your workplace and your friends as systems. Now decide:

• What parts of each system are open?
• What parts are closed?
• Why are some parts open and some closed?

• •

BOUNDARY MANAGEMENT

The divide between a system and the outside world is known as the **'boundary'** (see Figure 4). What occurs at the boundary of a system is vital to its life. It is not simply a line you step over, it is an area where a lot of activity takes place. The activity which goes on in the boundary area is called **boundary management**.

We all develop skills in boundary management as individuals. We decide quickly what kind of people we are going to be in different settings. We decide how much of ourselves we are prepared to share according to where we are and how much of what is happening around us is relevant to us.

You may not be conscious of the decisions you make regarding boundary management. Perhaps you are only reminded about the delicate issues of

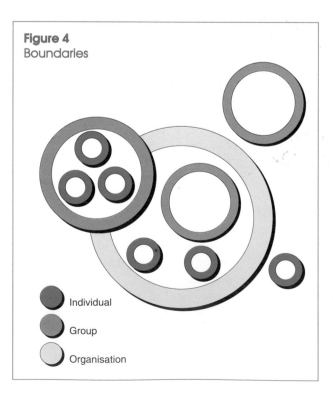

Figure 4
Boundaries

● Individual
● Group
○ Organisation

managing personal boundaries when you meet people who either embarrass you, by divulging highly personal material within minutes of your encounter with them, or frustrate you, by being so guarded that you never get to know them.

Boundary management also applies to groups and organisations. The boundary management of an open system determines the nature of both the input and the output. Imagine what would happen in a car manufacturing company, our example of an open system, if those responsible for input imported balsa wood instead of sheet metal, or those responsible for output failed to check reliability of the cars about to leave the factory.

What happens at the boundaries of a group affects its sense of safety and purposefulness. For example, if few outside influences are allowed in then the group becomes unproductive and directionless, but if all outside forces are allowed in then the group will be pushed and pulled in all directions, destroying the personal identity of group members and the strength of the group as a whole.

If, as a care worker, you work at the boundary of your group, and do business with other groups inside and outside your organisation, then you will have to work with other boundaries as well as those of your own group. For example, a group has to protect itself and give its members a sense of belonging so it must defend it boundary against outside forces which may make its members uncertain or fearful. These forces may come from another group which is also protecting its own boundary.

Neither individuals nor groups exist in isolation from one another. Groups inevitably become involved in activities with each other and whenever these activities take place the boundary of the group is threatened. This may lead to fears of loss of authority in the group and the possibility of chaos, as the example on the right shows.

See Exercise 27.

● ●

EXERCISE 27

Think of an occasion when you, or a group to which you belong, was being made to feel uncomfortable by another person or group.

- **What was going on at the boundary between you or your group and the other person or group?**
- **What steps did you take to protect yourself or your group?**

● ●

> ### *EXAMPLE*
>
> Shirley was a care worker in a day centre for people with learning difficulties. She was one of a group of staff who were becoming very upset about the way some of the clients were being treated by other members of staff. The staff Shirley and her group were concerned about had been working at the centre for over 15 years and were sure they knew everything there was to know about working with people with learning difficulties.
>
> Shirley decided to bring her concerns to the attention of the management group. The manager agreed with what she said, but seemed nervous about the issue being brought into the open. He suggested that Shirley spoke about it at the staff meeting. When Shirley raised the issue the staff whose methods were being questioned leapt to their own defence by criticising *her* (that is, they protected their boundary against invasion). The management group claimed to be neutral because they had to listen to both sides (that is, they protected their boundary). Shirley and her group felt unsupported and retreated (that is, they protected *their* boundary).
>
> Each group involved in this situation felt threatened and was only interested in making its point at the expense of other groups. There was now the risk of this resulting in a breakdown of group authority, which could lead to chaos and threaten the strength of the organisation.

While it is in the process of protecting its own boundary each group builds up a set of beliefs and perceptions about other groups. Groups do not usually check the accuracy of these beliefs but act towards other groups as if they were true.

For example, a group may believe that another group is less competent than it is and behave towards it as if this was true. This often happens in the management group of an organisation, when one of the team leaders is regarded as less competent than the others. He gets blamed for everything that goes wrong in the management group. In turn, his group gets blamed for everything which goes wrong in the organisation. Rather than

© CHURCHILL LIVINGSTONE 1992 (COPYING BY PERMISSION ONLY)

own up to our own incompetence we find it easier to find another individual or group to carry the responsibility for us.

If you work in a residential setting where the staff are divided into groups or teams – such as unit teams, day care staff or night care staff – try listening carefully to what your group says about the others, and what the others say about your group.

Try Exercise 28.

● ●

EXERCISE 28

Think of the various groupings in your workplace or social life.
- What do people in your group say about other groups?
- Do you consider that what they say is accurate?
- What do other groups say about your group?
- Do you think what they say is accurate?

● ●

DIFFERENT KINDS OF GROUPS

Think of a large group you have been with in a work situation (or even a group from school or college), and think of the way it is divided up into various smaller groups.

You will see immediately that people are divided up into groups according to the job or task that they have to carry out whether they are care staff, domestic staff, nursing staff, instructors, management, students or lecturers. In residential care settings people will also be divided up into shifts. For the sake of convenience we shall call these groups **work groups**.

If you look a little further you will also see other informal groupings. These groups form according to how people feel about one another and they may cut across the work groups. The basis of their coming together is some form of kinship or friendship where members tend to think alike about things in general and work issues in particular. They have a common feeling for each other and for this reason they are called **sentient** groups.

Sentient here means sharing a common awareness.

A sentient group might come together outside working hours, for example, going to the pub on a Friday after work. They may promise each other not to talk about work but they probably always do because it is their work that has brought them together. However, if the person in charge of the work group is also a member of a sentient group people are likely to say, 'There is no point in having staff meetings here. All the decisions get taken in the pub anyway!'

This raises serious issues about how the staff group works. On the one hand, the person in charge cannot forbid sentient groups and nor should she try to. It is perfectly natural for people with a common feeling for each other to come together. On the other hand, if the person in charge is guilty of making decisions about the unit only with her friends she is denying other members of staff their right to participate in decision-making. This situation is embarrassing if you happen to be a member of the sentient group and frustrating if you are not.

People should be able to acknowledge that they talk about work issues outside working hours and be absolutely open in staff meetings when ideas that began in a sentient group are being discussed at formal staff meetings.

The term 'sentient group' has been used rather than 'clique' because the word clique suggests secrecy, exclusiveness and potential unpleasantness. Sentient groups may turn into cliques if they are not open about their existence and what they discuss.

Sabotage groups consist of people who are so discontented with the way things are done in a unit that they want to bring the day-to-day running of the unit to a halt. A sabotage group can very quickly get through to a new member of staff or a student on placement. They pounce on the newcomer as he comes out of the office of the person in charge and say, 'Now we'll tell you what *really* goes on in this place!' People should be able to voice strong disagreement with the way in which a unit is run, but it is damaging to the unit if these disagreements go underground. The views of the saboteurs may be valid – the unit may genuinely need to be reorganised. If so, this should be brought out into the open.

5

Groups – internal processes

INSIDE A GROUP

Chapter 4 looked at the systems theory, which tries to describe what happens between and among groups. This chapter looks at what happens inside a group.

See Exercise 29.

● ●

EXERCISE 29

Think about your experiences as a member of a group:

- What is the group supposed to be doing?
- What is the group actually doing?
- Are the answers to these questions the same thing? If not, why not?

● ●

You may realise from trying Exercise 29 that there is sometimes a difference between what a group is *supposed* to be doing (the stated task) and what the group is *actually* doing (the actual task).

Why should groups be given one job and find themselves doing something quite different? Think about the work carried out in care settings, such as hospitals, day centres, residential homes or women's groups. The stated task of the workers is to look after the well-being of the patients, residents or attenders. Is this what they actually do? It may be that the workers are more concerned with looking after themselves than their clients. The use of phrases like, 'Watch your back', 'You've got to look after number one' or 'The routines here are more for the convenience of the staff than the residents' indicate that the attitude of the staff has shifted away from their clients.

Another way of looking at the situation where a group is trying to get on with the job stated, but seems to be carrying out a quite different task, is to consider **hidden agendas**. The hidden agenda is going on underneath the job the group is supposed to be doing.

In his book *Experiences in Groups* Wilfred Bion describes different kinds of hidden agenda:

- The dependent group
- The fight or flight group
- The pairing group

THE DEPENDENT GROUP

This term is used to describe a group which prefers to spend its time and energy finding a leader to take over its responsibilities rather than carrying out the job it has been given. The example in the panel on page 32 describes a dependent group.

THE FIGHT OR FLIGHT GROUP

This term describes a group which is either resisting doing the job it is supposed to do or running away from the task because it is scared. This sort of group uses statements like the following:

'This is ridiculous! We were given this job to do and no one knows how to do it!'

'How can management expect us to do this job when we don't even have enough staff on the ground?'

'This is far too much for us to do – we are just not up to it.'

EXAMPLE

A group of people was appointed from the clients and staff of an adult day care centre and given the job of organising social events in the centre. The clients expected one of the staff members to be in charge of the group. However, the staff member involved thought it would be more productive for the group if she didn't do everything. The group started to panic. They felt nervous about doing the job and instead directed their energies towards finding another leader. One of the clients was chosen and was so enthusiastic that he did everything himself, leaving very little for the rest of the group to do!

The hidden agenda in this situation was that this group was scared of getting on with its task so it looked for someone on whom it could depend to do the task for them.

A fight or flight group behaves as if its job is to find someone who will lead it into fighting against, or running away from, what it is supposed to be doing. Read the example in the panel again, but this time imagine that the group cannot find a client to come forward as leader. The group begins to get scared; some members express their views with statements like 'It's not fair that we've been asked to organise social events when no one will tell us what to do.' The group feel that the job is too much for them and that the staff are not being helpful – their hidden agenda is that they are fighting against organising social events or running away from the task.

THE PAIRING GROUP

Sometimes a group does not know what to do – everybody seems to wait for somebody else to take the lead. If 2 group members start to communicate and exchange views the other members are relieved because they might produce something that will come to the group's rescue. As a result, they pay the 2 members a lot of attention. In this case, the hidden agenda is that the group is relying on 2 people to get on with a task the whole group has been given.

Imagine again that the group in our example had failed to find a leader who would take over the work of the group. The group becomes angry and frightened. It tries either to fight against getting on with the job it has been set or it runs away from it. It then discovers that 2 people in the group are getting on well together and seem to know what should be done next. The group are happy to let these 2 people get on with the task set.

Try Exercise 30.

● ●

EXERCISE 30

Think of at least 3 groups of which you are a member, or with which you are familiar.
● Write down what you think the hidden agendas are for these groups. Can any of their hidden agendas be put into the categories of 'dependence', 'fight or flight', or 'pairing'?

● ●

A group's hidden agenda affects the ways in which the group operates. As individuals who will work in groups, and organise group activities, it is important that you understand what goes on in groups and are able to use this understanding to help the group achieve its task and operate in the most effective way. Most of us know what it is like to come away from a group or a meeting asking ourselves things like 'What was all that about? What is going on? We weren't getting on with the job in hand – we were caught up in something entirely different.'

USING THE HIDDEN AGENDA

Clearly, underlying processes are at work whatever the stated task of the group is. We can use these processes to help the group achieve its aim rather than get in the way of its purpose.

The following examples look at the 3 kinds of hidden agenda at work in groups from a children's home and consider ways in which each hidden agenda can be used to the groups' advantage.

DEPENDENCE

A care worker in the children's home was given the job of taking a group to the swimming baths. This was not the kind of trip she could let the group organise; she had to be responsible for all the arrangements.

The care worker expected the group to be dependent on her as leader. She knew that some group members would object to the way she organised things. She was prepared for them trying to influence the others in the group by 'fighting' against a swimming trip (because they said it was boring) or 'running away' from the idea (because they were scared). However, the care worker hoped that, if the majority of the group wanted the trip to go ahead, they would persuade the others that the best way to have a successful outing was to depend on her as leader.

The care worker was also responsible for the group's safety at the swimming pool so it was important that she was sure that they would follow her directions about behaviour.

In this situation, the more dependent the group was the more efficiently the stated task of the group would be achieved.

FIGHT OR FLIGHT

There was going to be a disco in the home. The disco committee had been working hard to arrange a good evening for everyone and had invited some young people from the local community to come along. However, these young people had been joined by some gatecrashers who had brought along a considerable amount of alcoholic drink. Soon a fight had broken out.

The disco committee members realised that it would not help to say, 'Right everybody, let's sit down and talk about this'! They restrained the people involved in the brawl ('fight') and got people away from the trouble ('flight').

The task was to have an enjoyable disco, but because that proved to be impossible the best course of action was to stop it by using 'fight' and 'flight'.

PAIRING

There had been several incidents of glue sniffing in the children's home. At first, the children found it very funny watching the staff rush around trying to take the glue from the sniffers, who wouldn't cooperate at all. The task of getting rid of the glue

and returning the home to normal seemed impossible.

However, 2 of the children became bored with all the attention being given to the sniffers. As far as they were concerned the novelty of the situation had worn off and they started objecting to what was going on. This had more influence on the glue sniffers than anything the staff had done.

The task was to get the whole group to work at stopping the glue sniffing but it was the work of 2 people which achieved it.

THE WORKING GROUP

Although we have been looking at ways to put hidden agendas to good use it is sometimes important for a group to work things out for itself. In certain situations, if a group falls back on its hidden agenda then it is avoiding what it is supposed to be doing.

Imagine, for example, that there has been a crisis at a training unit. A staff meeting is called and the group is given the task of solving the crisis. To do this all the members of the staff group have to take part. A number of things occur at the meeting:

- The head of the unit says, 'I know what's wrong. This is what we have to do . . . just follow me.' Everyone is relieved, until they find out that the head is not as sure about what to do as he says he is.
- Some group members say, 'This is too much; we can't cope. The whole thing is a disaster.' Many people agree with this view, but it doesn't move the group any closer to dealing with the crisis.
- Two people think they know the answer and follow a course of action. Again, the relief this brings is only shortlived and does not bring about a final resolution to the crisis.

Eventually, the group is forced to face up to its corporate (that is, shared) responsibility to get to grips with the crisis. Once individual members no longer expect others to do their work for them, they take back responsibility and authority for getting on with the job. When the group realise that they *can* do the job they set out to do they tackle it with renewed energy and feel much more confident when they finally succeed.

6

Working in groups

■ As a care worker the way you work with a group of people will differ from the way you work with separate individuals. When you are with an individual you are working with one person's perceptions and themes (see page 7). When you are with a group you are working with a number of people's perceptions and themes as they relate to you as a care worker and to each of the members of the group.

FORMAL AND INFORMAL GROUPS

When you work with groups it is important to distinguish between an informal group and a formal group. If you are with a group of children in a residential home at leisure time – watching television, playing pool, relaxing – you are not with a group, but you are there as a care worker with a group of children. This is called an **informal** group.

If the children decide to hold a table tennis competition then those taking part form a group with a job to do, and if you are involved your role changes too. This is called a **formal** group.

In other words, an informal group is a collection of individuals who happen to come together without any formal job to do. This kind of group may welcome group involvement but does not need anyone in the formal role of group worker. A formal group comes together deliberately to carry out a task and is therefore more likely to need a group worker who will have a formal role within the group.

THE TASK OF A GROUP

Once you know what kind of group you are with you must identify the task of the group so that you can decide what role you have in it. You may have to be a strong leader and direct the group, or you may have to avoid giving any kind of direction.

For example, if the group's task is to go hillwalking and you are an expert in this field then you would have the responsibility of getting the group up the hill and safely back down again. You would be the leader and would encourage the group to be dependent. However, if the group's task is to make up its mind on a particular course of action affecting the internal life of the group then you would *not* take over and tell them what to do.

See Exercise 31.

● ●

EXERCISE 31

The scene for this exercise is the workshop of a day care centre for adults with learning difficulties. One of the aims of the centre is to give clients help to understand social and group life.

A care worker at the centre is helping some of the adults in the workshop when a group of them begin to argue with one another. What do you think the care worker should do in this situation?

● ●

The situation described in Exercise 31 could provide a valuable learning experience for the clients. The care worker could rush in and sort things out by deciding herself who was wrong and who was right, but this would deprive members of the group of an important opportunity to learn about group life. It might also suppress certain members of the group, that is, they will feel put down by the force of authority represented by the care worker.

A care worker's task in this situation is to help members of the group gain a better understanding of what is happening to them and encourage them to sort things out for themselves.

FINDING AN ANSWER

Working in a group is a privileged position whether you are leading the group or a member of it. However, as a leader it is important that you neither patronise your group members nor treat them like children. You need to find the appropriate level of dependence for members according to the task the group has been given. There also has to be a balance between the leadership that comes from you and that which comes from other members of the group.

The greatest difficulty for people who work in formal or informal groups is to know 'where the answer lies'. A group asks a question and expects an answer, but where does the answer come from – the group itself, the leader or elsewhere?

AN ANSWER FROM THE GROUP

You may decide that a question can best be answered by letting the group come to its own conclusions. The example on the right describes how one key worker tackled this problem.

THE ANSWER IS WITH THE LEADER

If the answer is not available within the group then you, as a leader, have a responsibility to help the members of the group find the answer elsewhere. However, if you have the answer yourself you must not let the group know this and then tease them while they try to find it for themselves. Your relationship with the group members will suffer if you enjoy your superiority at their expense.

For example, returning to the situation described on the right, imagine how concerned the key worker would be if she discovered that the group members were so afraid of causing unpleasantness that they had decided not to take any action at all about the staff on the early shift. The key worker would have to take over

EXAMPLE

The key worker to a number of people in a home for elderly people held a meeting with them to discuss the situation regarding the day-to-day running of the home. One of the group complained that when a particular group of staff was on early shift it was very strict about getting the residents up in the morning.

The key worker knew that it was the home's policy to allow residents to have long lies if they wanted, within reason. She also knew that the answer to this complaint would be to take it to the head of the home, who was a very approachable person.

The group started to discuss what it was going to do. Some people wanted to take their complaint 'to the very top'; some didn't want to do this because it would cause unpleasantness; others didn't think the problem was 'all that serious, anyway'.

If the key worker told the group that the answer was to alert the head of the home to the situation she would be:

- denying the group the chance to decide for itself
- suggesting that members of the group were unable to work things out and decide on a course of action
- suggesting to the group that she was the only one who could do anything

The key worker decided to be patient and she:

- encouraged the group to explore the nature of the problem
- helped people to understand all the factors which had to be taken into consideration
- got the group to explore why certain members were fearful.

This exploration gave the group confidence to make a decision and act on it.

responsibility as leader because the group could not come to an appropriate conclusion.

In this instance, the key worker could say that, in her opinion, the problem was a serious one and should not be abandoned. She could explain that

© CHURCHILL LIVINGSTONE 1992 (COPYING BY PERMISSION ONLY)

the head of the home would want to know about the residents' grievance because it was against the policy of the home not to allow them a long lie. She could also assure them that there was no need to be frightened of anyone being blamed for the results of their action and offer to accompany members of the group to see the head.

THE ANSWER LIES ELSEWHERE

It may be that neither the group nor the leader can supply the answer. If the key worker in our example agreed that individual residents or staff might be blamed or accused if the matter was brought to the head, then the responsibility to take action would lie entirely with her, as a member of staff. It would be inappropriate to expect the group to deal with a problem which belongs to a staff group.

KEEPING THE GROUP GOING

People working in groups spend a lot of time deciding who has the responsibility for keeping the group going. If a group starts losing interest in its task the group worker may feel responsible and react by encouraging people to be more enthusiastic. If your role is that of instructor or teacher it is your responsibility to keep interest alive. But if your job in the group is to help it take responsibility for its own work then if you revive flagging enthusiasm you may be doing so because you are anxious about the way the group is going, rather than working out what is preventing the group from getting on with its business. However, the group may genuinely be stuck and need your help. You have the difficult job of working out whether the dependent needs expressed by the group require you to act as rescuer, or if the group is trying to get you to do its job for it.

WORKING WITH SILENCE

Everyone who takes part in a group, both group leaders and group members, is terrified of silence! A group may fall into silence because it is embarrassed; if members do not know what to say, or what is happening, they can be left staring at the floor in discomfort.

Yet silence can be respectful, healing, productive and caring. Group members may cover up their real feelings by talking about anything and everything; in this situation both the leader and

> **EXAMPLE**
>
> One of the men in a discussion group admitted that he disliked being made to look inferior by other men and, because he reacted this way, he felt very aggressive towards the male group worker leading the group. The group had only been meeting for a short time and avoided dealing with this powerful statement by ignoring it. The group worker made no comment.
>
> The group moved on to talk about other things. Eventually, they discussed the reasons why some group members tended to remain silent. Some members said that people could be silent if they wanted to because 'it's their choice – it's not up to the rest of us to force them to talk.' Others agreed, but suddenly a group member blurted out that she was silent because she was afraid of the power and position of the group worker. The group became very quiet and the group worker decided to comment. He reminded the group of the earlier remark a member had made about the rivalry with himself and linked it with the silent lady's comment. This time the group did not ignore the statement and the whole group spoke out about their feelings towards the group worker and how they were going to deal with them.

other members can find themselves wishing that the others would be quiet and allow everybody the peace to think about what has happened.

If you have responsibility for the way a group develops you have to decide what to do with silences. You should only start talking if you know what the silence is about, not just because you feel uncomfortable. Remember your task is to help the group get on with its job.

WHEN TO START TALKING

For a group leader, dealing with too much noise can be just as difficult as dealing with silence! Sometimes group members are talking about so many different things that you do not know which to respond to. You may be tempted to stop the group so that you can make your comments, but try *not* to do this. If you let the group continue talking you will find that members of the group will make the points you would have made.

It can be difficult not to make your contributions because you, as leader, need to feel useful to the group. If group members voice all *your* thoughts and observations you may feel like a spare part! Instead, give yourself credit for having the skill to allow the group members to express these ideas.

However, there may be times when you wait patiently for other people to pick up on something which you think is important, but the group drifts away from the issue or tries to avoid it. If this happens you must draw the group's attention to the point it is missing, For example, a group member may say something significant and you hold back, expecting someone else in the group to pick up on the statement. If no one does, and the group wanders off in another direction, you might worry that the opportunity to discuss something important has been lost. However, it is quite likely that someone else has stored up this information and that the discussion will return to something similar. When this happens you will be able to link it with the earlier statement, as in the example given on page 36.

Now try Exercise 32.

While completing Exercise 32 you may have thought, 'This is ridiculous! I'm not a trained group worker, I'm a care worker.' This is true, but nevertheless care workers can be key workers, they do work with groups – including reminiscence groups. Care workers can be involved in groups where all kinds of things happen and they need to know how to react.

Exercise 32 gives you a chance to think about how you might behave in a particular group, especially when you are working with a colleague.

EXERCISE 32

(Whenever you come across an asterisk * in this exercise pause and write down what you should say and do at that point in the meeting.)

Imagine that you and a fellow care worker have set up a reminiscence group of elderly people, to share memories and talk about past events. After two or three meetings the group seems to be going well until you notice that, during an ordinary conversation, one of the group members has started crying. At first, only some of the group members notice it.

How would you feel when you first notice that a group member was crying?*

Suddenly, everyone in the group realises that one member is in tears and the conversation stops. Some members look away, embarrassed. Others look at you and your colleague to see what you will do. One member tries to comfort the person in tears by putting his arm around her. But she draws away and says, 'It's all right. Please just leave me alone and carry on. I'll be fine in a minute.'

How do you react to this?*

Because they feel so awkward the group tries to carry on talking, but one member is un-happy about this and says, 'I'm really very worried about Betty. Surely we can't just carry on as if there was nothing wrong with her?' The group goes silent again and some of them look at you to see what you are going to do.*

Eventually, Betty is able to tell the group that the earlier conversation reminded her of the time her husband was killed in an industrial accident. Members of the group start apologising for having stirred up memories of that painful time.*

One of the group members now becomes very agitated and says, 'This is awful – I can't bear it. I think I'll need to leave.' Again, members of the group look at you and your colleague.* People in the group try to persuade the member to stay, but she starts to get up out of her chair.* Then she changes her mind and sits down again. The group is silent once more.*

The mood of the group has changed. They had been exchanging pleasant memories and jokes about the 'good old days', but Betty's intervention has reminded them of the more serious side of life. The group's members are elderly, but they are also individuals with their own thoughts and opinions about their experience of life. How does this change of mood make you feel?*

© CHURCHILL LIVINGSTONE 1992 (COPYING BY PERMISSION ONLY)

37

If you have time, go through the exercise again and think of alternative responses to the ones you wrote down at each asterisk.

It is useful to have some idea of the most appropriate things to say and do in a reminiscence group. There are many factors to consider when you are deciding whether to remain silent or come in with a comment. Remember, there are times when someone says something so important that the best response is silence. Often, all the members of a group recognise this and remain silent too. However, one group member might be so overwhelmed by what has been said that he leaps in with reassuring, but inappropriate, remarks. At first, you should continue to be silent because another member might say something to stop the flow of nervous remarks. If this does not happen, and you can see that the member who made the original statement is becoming distressed by the reassurances, you may have to draw attention to the fact.

WHEN GROUP MEMBERS CRY

When people burst into tears they often say, 'I'm sorry about all this.' In other words they are apologising to the group members for upsetting them. Typical responses to a person bursting into tears are:

'There, there, don't upset yourself so. Everything will be fine.'

The person saying this cannot cope with the other person crying and would like them to stop as soon as possible.

'There, there, it's all right for you to cry.'

The person saying this is *saying* that it is all right for the person to cry, but the reassuring words are concealing the fact that he is unsure about how to deal with the situation.

'Please go on talking through your tears.'

If the person saying this looks over and listens rather than talks then she is conveying that she is able and willing to hear more. She can express her interest by confirming this in words.

If crying occurs when you are working in a group, look around to see if anyone in the group will be able to respond in this way. If there *is* someone you must stay silent and let him speak. You must only speak out if no one else is able to.

See Exercise 33.

EXERCISE 33

The following incident occurred in a children's home.

A group of children, and a care worker, were watching a soap opera on television. During a scene showing marital violence one of the children made a laughing remark. Suddenly, one of the girls burst into tears and the following exchange took place:

'Just what do you mean by that?' she cried.
'Don't be daft,' said the boy. 'I was only joking.'
'What's so funny about it then?' the girl retorted.
'Oh, shut up!' said the boy.
'I will not shut up! What do you know about it anyway?' the girl shouted.

- If you had been the care worker how would you have reacted to this situation? What would you have said and done?

The girl became very upset and soon other children from the group became involved. They found out that one of the reasons the girl was in the children's home was because there was a lot of violence in her own home. The care worker already knew this.

- As a care worker what would you have said and done once the other children knew the girl's background?

Exercise 33 shows what happens when an unexpected occurrence turns a collection of people into a group. The care worker could have responded by taking the girl away from the group and talking to her privately. This would have been appropriate but would have brought the new group to an end and denied them the opportunity to think and talk about what had just happened.

If you can, go over Exercise 33 again and think of a different set of responses – what would the consequences of *these* actions be?

When a group member bursts into tears other members may immediately look to you for guidance on how to respond. This can be particularly difficult if you too feel like crying because you identify closely with what the group member has been saying. However, it is not your job to cry – let fellow members cry with each other. Your job is to let the group know that it is perfectly acceptable for *them* to cry.

As group leader, you want the group to feel safe enough to talk about distressing emotions. One way to do this is to maintain a confident silence. A confident silence shows that you understand what is happening, can feel for the other person's pain without losing control, and that you can give the other group members strength to work with the pain being expressed.

The other way to make the group feel safe is for you, or another group member, to encourage the person to keep talking through his tears.

SPEAKING OUT

Sometimes, every member of a group avoids expressing what obviously needs to be said because they think it would upset people and cause further difficulties. You have to decide whether anyone in the group should speak out or if it is your job to do so.

See Exercise 34.

· ·

EXERCISE 34

A health care assistant (HCA) in a day hospital regularly attended the weekly staff meeting. During one meeting, the staff were told that a relative of a lady at the day hospital had made a serious complaint about the way her mother had been treated by a particular member of staff. The member of staff in question loudly denied this and was supported by her friends.

The HCA felt anxious because she had seen the way this staff member usually behaved and knew the complaint to be true. She looked at the nurse in charge, who seemed uncertain. The HCA also felt uncomfortable because she knew that the member of staff concerned, and her friends, were a powerful sub-group within the staff. However, she also knew that many staff members were concerned about this sub-group because its members treated the day patients roughly and without respect.

The HCA waited to see if any other staff members felt as she did – perhaps, like her, they did not feel able to speak out. What about the nurse in charge – did she really know what went on in the staff group? If she did, it was up to her to deal with the woman who was the subject of the complaint. If the nurse in charge hadn't got the courage to do this then who would?

The HCA was in a dilemma. She knew the complaint was justified and that no one should be allowed to go on treating patients in this way. But if others knew the complaint was justified why should *she* be the one to speak out?

What do you think the HCA should do?:

· Keep her feelings to herself and say, and do, nothing. She is a main grade worker so it is up to the supervisors to do something about the situation.

· Try to catch the eye of someone who agrees with her, judge what she is thinking and silently hint that the other person should be the one to speak out.

· Say nothing until the staff meeting is over, then make a point of talking to her immediate supervisor in the hope that she will have the courage to take the matter further.

· Start to speak, making clear (even if the words tumble out nervously) that the complaint is justified and has to be dealt with.

· ·

There are disadvantages to all the options given in Exercise 34, for example:

- **If the HCA did not do anything the unacceptable practice would continue and she would feel guilty about not having had the courage of her convictions. She could not be sure that her supervisors would have the courage to do something.**
- **If the HCA spoke to her supervisor after the meeting, and told her it was *her* job to take the matter further, she would be at a disadvantage because she would be on her own without any backing from others in the group. Alternatively, she could speak directly to the supervisor at the meeting and say, 'I think you should say something about this.'**
- **If the HCA decided, 'I've had enough of this – if nobody else is going to speak out then I will' she would run the risk of being victimised by the powerful sub-group.**

If you were a group leader in a situation like this, and could see all that is going on in the group, you might be able to help the HCA say what needs to be said. If the nurse in charge was able to notice and understand the HCA's discomfort she could:

- **Find a way of helping the HCA say what she wants to say.**
- **Realise that it is not the HCA's job to say anything and take on the responsibility for speaking herself.**

WORKING WITH A CO-WORKER

When you have a co-worker *you must both agree on the task of the group* – the group will be thoroughly confused if you each have different ideas about what the group should be doing. A group responds very strongly for or against its leaders. Whether you and your co-worker are of the same sex or not, one of you will probably become the 'mother' of the group and the other the 'father'. (This is quite normal – see the section on projection and transference on pages 6 and 7).

Once you have agreed on the task of the group *you can then agree to work together*. The role of group worker is potentially threatening to the members of the group because they think it has special qualities and they are fearful of it. A group feels even more overwhelmed if it is faced with *2* group workers! It may want to cause a division

between them to reduce their powers.

You have to acknowledge that these forces are at work, but you must not defend yourselves by combining against the group. Even if you feel that the group is uniting against you, you must be seen to be working together *without* giving the impression that only the *2* of you know what is really going on. You must allow members to give expression to the whole range of their experience.

ALLOWING EXPRESSION

When one of you is contributing to a particular part of the discussion the other should not immediately follow it with her own idea. Don't use your co-worker as a way of coming in yourself – wait for an appropriate time instead.

There will be times when you and your co-worker have differing views about what is going on in the group. It is important that you are both able to express your difference of opinion. It is all right to disagree with each other in a way which reflects a disagreement which has occurred in the group itself.

Avoid talking with your co-worker and leaving the group to look on. The group might be delighted to let you get on with the task – in other words, they can fall into the hidden agenda of pairing.

Don't behave towards one another as if you are sharing a secret. For example, group members find it very unsettling if their 2 group workers are in the habit of giving each other knowing looks.

It is important to talk to each other at the end of each group session – even about your individual views on what happened in the group and about the way you are both working together. The discussion should include questions like:

- **What role is each of you taking in the group?**
- **What kind of material is being transferred to you by group members?**
- **Do the group members see both of you as being frightening or helpful?**
- **Have there been any disagreements between you which have not been raised by the group itself, and which you need to resolve outside the group?**
- **Are the influences which you bring to bear on the group positive or negative?**

Working with groups may not always be such a complicated business! If a group is tackling a straightforward task you are not likely to become involved in the kind of detail described in this chapter. The important thing is to make sure that the group – whether or not it develops into a simple or a complex group – is achieving its aims.

If the task of the group is to make something – for example, an arts and crafts group – then your job is to help it carry this out. You must resist the temptation to do things for the group. You do not need to get involved with the comings and goings of the group members, although it is useful to take note of them – you may need to use your knowledge of group behaviour if it is preventing the group from completing its task.

If the task of the group is to sort something out – for example, people in a small living unit who are tackling issues of living together – then your job is to listen to what is happening and use your understanding to help them achieve a resolution to their difficulties.

Human behaviour in groups is complex, but it is important that you don't think it is a very mysterious subject. We all live and work in groups every day of our lives. Your experience and knowledge of living and working in groups will be of great use to you when you take on the role of group worker. Take the time to think about your own experiences and use them when your job is to understand what is happening in a group. If you are able to trust your own judgement, and use it constructively, you will not be so anxious about working in groups. However experienced you are there is always more to learn, especially from unexpected occurrences. Each group you work with is unique, and now and then one of them is bound to spring a surprise on you!

PRACTICAL PREPARATION

This chapter has covered a wide range of situations in which you may find yourself as part of a group – as participant, facilitator, leader or instructor. There will be occasions when you are responsible for running a group, perhaps on a visit or outing, at a sports or games session, for discussion or at a meeting. Your groups should run more smoothly if you consider the following practical questions beforehand:

- **Are you clear about the task, or purpose, of the group?**
- **Are you clear about which role you, or any colleagues, will take in the group?**
- **Do you know who is coming to the group?**
- **What steps have you taken to make sure that those who are coming to the group know what the group is for?**
- **Have you told members when the group starts and finishes?**
- **Have you prepared the room, or any other spaces required, for the purposes of the group? For example, do you need chairs, warmth or privacy?**
- **If the group is to be involved in activities have you made sure that the necessary equipment is in place?**
- **Even though it is not your responsibility to make the experience of the group a pleasant one for members, have you made sure that their basic physical needs are catered for?**

You are responsible for managing the boundary of the group and making sure that you have created a setting where the group can get on with its work. One of the most important parts of this job is the management of time. People feel anxious if they do not know the starting and finishing times of a group.

This is not a complete list of all the preparations necessary for a group, but you can use it as a guideline and add your own points as they arise. The Suggested Reading list at the end of the book includes some material which will help you add details to this framework.

You may find the sumary of 'Dos and don'ts in a group' on page 42 provides you with a useful checklist of the main points covered in this chapter.

DOS AND DON'TS IN A GROUP

- Do decide why you are working in a group rather than with individuals.
- Do decide whether you are working with a formal or informal group.
- Do be alert to occasions when an informal group changes to a formal group and adapt the way you are working.
- Do decide what level of dependence it is appropriate for the group to have.
- Do try to be aware of where the answer can be found.
- Don't jump in too fast with the answer or you may be stopping the group from finding the answer itself.
- Do think about whether it is your job to keep the group going. If it isn't, don't speak out just because you are anxious.
- Do try to get used to silence. Once you are comfortable with silence you will find it easier to know when to break the silence and when you should keep quiet.
- Don't voice your opinion all the time. You may have opinions on everything being raised, but it may not be appropriate for *you* to express them – let others do that. Also, when someone says something you would have said don't say, 'You know, I was just about to say that myself!' Instead, feel pleased that you gave someone else the chance to say it by keeping quiet.
- Do take the responsibility to say or do something, if it is necessary.

- Do try to become more comforable when people cry in your groups. Instead of being upset or embarrassed, work out what the crying is about and then decide on the best course of action.
- Do work out who should 'speak out' in the group you are in. If you are sure it is not your job then remain silent; if your are sure it *is* your job then have the courage to speak.
- When with a co-worker:

   - Do agree on the task of the group.
   - Do be alert to the negative and positive feelings the group has about you both.
   - Do be aware of what the group may be trying to do to you, such as split you up and play one of you against the other.
   - Don't unite against the group.
   - Don't use what your co-worker says to leap straight in with your opinions.
   - Do express a different view if you hold it but don't end up arguing with each other.
   - Don't give each other knowing looks, as if you are sharing a secret no one in the group knows about.
   - Do take time to talk together after the group is over.

- Do treat groups with respect but don't be frightened of them.

CONCLUSION

This book is about working with people, families and groups, but it is also about you because as soon as you think about, and work with, other peoples' lives you are likely to be reminded of your own experiences. We have tried to help you in your work with other people by showing you how to use your own experience of life in a balanced way. It is important to find a balance between not allowing any of your own experience to come into your work, and not becoming so caught up with your own experience that you have no room left for involvement in other people's lives. This is always a difficult balance to achieve.

Many of the exercises are about you and your life. You may have enjoyed some of them but others may have disturbed you. Do not worry if this has been the case – most people are disturbed about some part of their lives. In fact, being in touch with what disturbs you – as well as what interests you and gives you joy – is a sign that you are continuing to grow as a person.